# Healing the Gender Wars

## Therapy with Men and Couples

**Samuel Slipp, M.D.**

JASON ARONSON INC.
*Northvale, New Jersey*
*London*

This book was set in 11 pt. New Century Schoolbook by Alpha Graphics of Pittsfield, New Hampshire, and printed and bound by Book-mart Press of North Bergen, New Jersey.

**Library of Congress Cataloging-in-Publication Data**

Slipp, Samuel.
    Healing the gender wars : therapy with men and couples /
by Samuel Slipp.
        p.   cm.
    Includes bibliographical references and index.
    ISBN 1–56821–773–0 (alk. paper)
    1. Men—Mental health.   2. Object relations (Psychoanalysis)
3. Man–woman relationships.   4. Psychotherapy.   I. Title.
    [DNLM:   1. Object Attachment.   2. Men—psychology.   3. Behavior
Therapy.   WM 460.5.02 S633h 1996]
RC451.4.M45S56   1996
616.89'14'081—dc20
DNLM/DLC
for Library of Congress                                              95-46925

Manufactured in the United States of America. Jason Aronson Inc. offers books and cassettes. For information and catalog write to Jason Aronson Inc., 230 Livingston Street, Northvale, New Jersey 07647.

# Healing the Gender Wars

*Dedicated to*

*My father, William Slipp*

*My wife, Sandra*

*My daughter, Elena*

# Contents

# Introduction

There is an ancient Chinese curse that states, "May you live in interesting times." Changing times are interesting times. Emile Durkheim, the eminent sociologist, found that this curse was scientifically accurate. He noted that when values and norms change in society, there is an increase in emotional disturbances and suicide. On the other hand, the philosopher Friedrich Nietzsche stated in *Thus Spake Zarathustra* (Durant 1926, p. 464) that social strife and turmoil may destroy some but may bring out the latent greatness in others. He wrote, "Out of such chaos comes the dancing star." We are now in the throes of this mixed curse/blessing, as society is currently undergoing a radical change. Thus there is a great need for mental health professionals to help those who fall by the wayside and to facilitate the growth of those who are able to use this stimulus for greater enrichment in their lives.

Probably the most damaging effect of social stress today is the breakdown of a sense of community. There are challenges to the traditional authority structure of society and of the family. On a personal level, this is demonstrated by more overt conflicts between the genders, a greater fear of commitment by men, and increased violence and abuse within marriage. About one-third of children are now born out of wedlock in the United States and England, and half of the marriages end in divorce. As a result of gender conflict, more and more men are entering psychotherapy, either of their own volition or at the urging of the women with whom they have a relationship. Many other men, especially those over 45, come for professional help because of anxiety, depression, and marital conflict resulting from loss of their jobs as we enter a postindustrial society that is lean and mean. This book is an attempt to identify the current problems that face men in our rapidly changing society and to help therapists heal the gender war in individual and couples therapy.

## CONSISTENCY OF THEORY AND THERAPY

Many books about psychotherapy with men contain a glaring internal inconsistency between theory and therapy. They mention the sociological changes that have occurred, but use only one theory of gender development, which is psychoanalytic. The authors defensively apologize for using analytic theory, then maintain an antianalytic stance and employ educational or behavioral techniques in therapy. They seem to believe that logic and persuasion will offer a quick way to change men's behavior, and do not take into account the deeply ingrained influences from childhood. This book also takes into account the impact of social changes, but employs a theory of gender development and a therapeutic approach that is psychoanalytic to provide consistency.

The question is, why has there been such bias against psychoanalytic theory and therapy? One can look at family therapy as an example, since it has been largely antianalytic from its beginnings. In the United States, family therapy developed during the Vietnam war years, when political movements against authority arose and postmodern philosophy developed. The only general theory that was acceptable was a theory about theories (Slipp 1994).

Tracing the evolution of family therapy in its cultural context, Frank Pittman (1992, pp. 9, 25) admits that the "open defiance of psychoanalytic postures . . . represent[s] subtle defiance of the patriarchal hierarchy still in effect." Pittman states that family therapists originally blamed women in the l950s, parents in the 1960s, adult responsibilities that inhibited freedom in the 1970s, and patriarchal society and men in the 1980s. Pittman then notes that the result of our "postpatriarchal" society has men finding their masculinity in "escaping commitment, sexual victories over women, and in violent victories over men." Women find "female affirmation by escaping patriarchal marriages, proving they don't need men to live fulfilling lives."

Even though Pittman recognizes the rebellion against patriarchal authority, he and many other therapists simplistically scapegoat psychoanalysis for what he calls the "mess"—the "destruction of the family," and the "self-indulgent and violent society." Blaming psychoanalysis for everything that is wrong is preposterous, because it ignores economic, political, social, and technological changes that have shaped modern society. It is analogous to some politicians' blaming unmarried mothers on welfare for all the economic problems that currently exist. It is also erroneous to state that we have arrived at a postpatriarchal society. There are only eight women in the U.S. Senate, a seat of political power, and only 5 percent of top executives are women, according to the recent Federal Glass Ceiling Commission report (1995). Throughout the corporate world women, blacks, and Latinos earn less than white men for the same work. Women are still struggling to get equal pay with men for equal work.

Clearly psychoanalysis cannot be set up as a straw man and blamed for all the problems of the family and society. As Pittman notes (1992), searching for blame, switching from one scapegoat to another, has not been productive. Since problems with fathers have been extensive in our society, one wonders if unresolved father conflicts have been displaced onto psychoanalysis. Understanding, not blaming, accepting complexity, not resorting to reductionism, are the answers.

Psychoanalysis itself is part of the transition of society from a communal to a more individualistic culture, which will be described in Chapter 1. Psychoanalysis helped free women and men from sexual repression and, by focusing on individual feelings and conflicts, helped lift people from constricted, stereotyped roles. Because the cohesion of the family and society has been lessened by this general cultural transition, human attachment has become the central issue. It is therefore fitting that object relations psychoanalytic theory, which focuses on human attachment, will be employed both diagnostically and therapeutically. As used here, it provides a bridge between social, familial, interpersonal, and intrapsychic systems. Object relations theory asserts that human bonding, not sex or aggression, is the most important factor in personality development. It is supported scientifically by animal studies, such as Harry Harlow's (1958) monkey experiments, in which attachment was found to be more significant than feeding. Direct infant observational studies, such as Daniel Stern's work (1985), noted the crucial developmental significance of early bonding and attunement of mother and child.

There has also been criticism of psychoanalysis as a science by Adolph Grünbaum (1993) and others because analytic research is based on clinical case studies. Lloyd Silverman (1975), however, developed a scientific laboratory method to validate psychoanalytic theory, especially internalized object relations. In a double-blind procedure, a tachistoscope flashes verbal and pictorial messages so fast that it bypasses consciousness and activates unconscious fantasies. The effects can be measured by tests of thought, affect, self-object differentiation, and so on. Silverman found that with schizophrenic patients the message of "Mommy and I Are One" reduced thought disorder, but only if the subject had sufficiently differentiated from the mother.

We (Slipp and Nissenfeld 1981) employed this laboratory method with forty-eight neurotically depressed women and found that this same maternal symbiotic message improved their depression. But, if the mother was experienced and internalized as pressuring and invasive, and did not gratify success, this subliminal message was ineffective. A second message, "Succeed for Yourself," was also ineffective, because autonomy was equated with abandonment.

In another tachistoscopic study of 108 underachieving high-school students, Greenberg (1980) and I (Slipp 1988) used this procedure therapeutically four times a week for six weeks. We found this maternal symbiotic message effective in increasing boys' grades, but only if the mother was experienced and internalized as gratifying and not invasive. In girls, only the subliminal message of "My Success Is OK" gave them permission to succeed academically and increased their attachment to their fathers. This latter message was also effective in boys who had experienced and internalized conflicted maternal relations. These boys scored high for fear of autonomy and fear of success on psychological tests. On posttesting the maternally conflicted boys also felt closer to their fathers, and seemed to gain permission to succeed.

Object relations theory and therapy deal not only with how early attachments are internalized, but also with how separation and individuation lead to an autonomous personality. The child's striving for growth and mastery must be responded to appropriately by parents to suit the child's needs. Boundary violations and establishing a taboo against separation by parents can result in symbiotic relatedness and pathology, while insufficient or conflictual attachment can produce inferior functioning, and pathology as well. The above empirical laboratory studies validate the findings noted in clinical case studies.

Besides the family's specific dynamics, gender stereotypes, as defined by the culture, are also internalized into the self. The family also transmits cultural stereotypes, which are incorporated by the child to form its core gender identity (Stoller 1968). A stereotype is defined as attributing a characteristic to all members of a group, although the degree of internalization of this cultural value varies with the individual. For example, some men conform to the macho stereotype and need to dominate, compete, and control. This is not inevitable, however, since not all men display these characteristics. Core gender identity is fixed around 3 years of age, and the child defines himself or herself in terms of feeling masculine or feminine. Around this time, firmer ego boundaries are also established, so that self and object constancy occur. Thus, a consistent and permanent sense of self and other is established; the child can tolerate separation, and is less dependent on others to sustain its self-esteem and identity.

Either because of genetic deficit, invasiveness by the family, or conforming to cultural stereotype, the achievement of separation and autonomy may be disrupted. In certain cultures one child is designated to devote his or her life to the parents. In some families a parent may use a child as an extension of himself or herself for his or her own personality needs; the child's drive for separating and establishing ego boundaries may thus be disrupted. Children comply to this invasion for their own security, because their survival is at stake. They fear abandonment if they are autonomous, and thus do not achieve a sense of confidence and mastery with independence. The invasion of ego boundaries can be compared to one nation's not respecting the integrity of another nation and invading it to satisfy its own needs.

Object relations provided a theoretical basis for my clinical research at New York University–Bellevue Medical Center. I (Slipp 1984, 1988) found four types of family structures that prevented separation and individuation, which were related to four types of psychopathology. Normally, an optimal degree of cohesiveness and differentiation exists in the family. Each person then gains support and nurturance from the togetherness and can have a separate life of his or her own. In the families studied group cohesion was preserved, but at the expense of individual boundaries. The family was not a safe and supportive sanctuary but a stifling and confining prison.

This process of support and freedom in the family is similar to what happens in object relations therapy with individuals, couples, and families. The therapist creates an optimal condition for bonding and autonomy, so that a safe holding environment is established in which differentiation can occur. The therapist empathically serves as a container for the patient's projective identifications, experiences them, and tries not to be induced to enact the patient's projections. For example, a male patient may try to project his own feelings of inadequacy by trying to make the therapist feel inadequate. The therapist needs to be aware of and contain his or her countertransference reactions and to use them as a therapeutic tool instead of becoming defensive or angry. The therapist maintains autonomy, metabolizes the patient's projections, and offers them as an interpretation of the unconscious conflicts within the person, couple, or family. In the example above, the therapist might acknowledge feeling inadequate, yet wonder if there is something the patient is struggling with, and needs to share this feeling so that the therapist can empathically understand him better. This helps differentiate the therapist from the patient's internal images of the self or other, yet it is reframed into a noncritical statement. Boundaries are thereby established between internal representations and external reality; between the self and others. In addition to differentiation, self and object constancy is secured and symbolic functioning is facilitated. Further growth of the patient can occur within this trusting and empathic framework. The patient recognizes and reowns his conflicts within a safe holding environment and can work through unacceptable aspects that were previously projected into others.

The projective identification process is especially important for gender issues, since traditional culture itself invaded the boundaries between the genders. Aspects of men that were considered weak were unconsciously split off and projected into women. Women served as containers and were induced to enact these unacceptable personality traits of men. These unacceptable traits included emotionality, dependence, helplessness, and vulnerability. Men then could feel that they were the rational ones, independent, masterful, and invulnerable. Only by reowning these projections can true equality between the sexes be achieved to heal the gender wars.

# 1

# Gender Wars as Society Changed from Being Communal to Individualistic

## TRADITIONAL SOCIETY

Society in the Western world has gradually changed from a traditional communal structure to one that is more individualistic, where people now feel entitled to "do their own thing." In traditional society most people gained social acceptance, self-esteem, and identity by satisfying the expectations and rules of the national, ethnic, or religious group to which they belonged. Individuals were bound together tightly in the community by the shackles of moral restraint and duty as advocated by the group's religious and social values. Lack of conformity to these values resulted in social ostracism, exclusion, or death. Executions were held in public as another way of externally reinforcing the community's values.

The punishment for deviation from the group's values has gradually lessened through the ages, and controls changed from external to internal. Examples drawn from the Bible and literature will be used to illustrate the changing cultural belief systems. In the New Testament,

Mary Magdalene had committed the sin of adultery and was condemned to death by public stoning, only to be rescued by a more individualistic and humanistic Jesus. In *The Scarlet Letter*, a novel of early Puritan New England by Nathaniel Hawthorne, Hester Prynne, who also committed adultery, was physically excluded from society. She was punished by having to stand and hold her child on the platform of the pillory and to wear a badge of shame, the letter A, embroidered on her dress. In Edith Wharton's novel *The Age of Innocence*, the Victorian hero was conflicted between rebelling or conforming to society, and chose the latter to avoid loss of social status.

The nonconformist in a communal culture usually experienced shame. Since individual identity and self-esteem depended greatly on how the group perceived them, people were very concerned about what others in the community thought. Conformity was essential in a communal culture, because it was necessary for people in an agricultural or hunting society to work together as a group to ensure survival for all. Members of the group were interdependent and strictly bound together by reciprocal obligations. Nonconformity was seen as a betrayal of the group, resulting in exclusion or punishment. Individual identity was defined by the community and often was reflected in the family surname that described their function in society. A person whose family name was Smith was a blacksmith, and one who was called Weaver was a weaver. Conformity provided an identity, enhanced self-esteem, defined gender relations, and brought acceptance by the community. The extended family and community made up civil society and provided support, mastery, and security to its members who were dependent upon one another.

## THE INDUSTRIAL REVOLUTION

What are some of the changes in society that the therapist needs to be aware of? Even though some of these factors may be familiar to many readers, it may be of use to summarize them. This may lead to clarification of some misconceptions, since some groups erroneously blame the feminist movement for the current problems in the family and society, which is simplistic and regressive, and uses splitting to set up a scapegoat. Blaming results in premature closure of uncertainty and a paranoid attitude where the other is demonized. This only polarizes gender relations into oppressor and victim. Problems about the breakdown of the solidarity of the community and the family in civil society need to be understood as the result of a number of historical and economic factors.

As the agricultural society gave way to the Industrial Revolution in the eighteenth century, people moved from small towns to large cities. The countryside became less populated and social supports from family solidarity and a sense of community were diminished or destroyed. Men could no longer be identified as a member of a particular artisan group or as a farmer from a particular small town. The result was an identity crisis for men especially. It was no longer feasible for the family and artisans to produce material goods by simple hand tools and physical labor. Factories, using power-driven machines, resulted in men's labor being less differentiated. Particular skills were no longer necessary, since machines manufactured products more efficiently and cheaply. Factory workers performed the same operation on assembly lines and were not responsible for the finished product. Although more people were able to have greater material comfort due to mass production, skilled craftsmen could no longer take pride in or define themselves in terms of their particular work.

For example, one of the consequences at the turn of the century in Vienna was that displaced artisans formed the Society for the Defense of the Handworker (Slipp 1993). Their frustration and powerlessness resulted in regression, group merging, and expressions of anger at a common enemy. This is a primitive adaptation in order to establish meaning and mastery that I have called the *symbiotic survival pattern* (Slipp 1973; see also Chapter 4). Autonomy is sacrificed for survival of the group. Here, individual boundaries are dissolved to gain group support, and others are seen only as members of a group. In Vienna, antiliberal and anti-Semitic scapegoating resulted, which was used by demagogues to gain political power. Two examples are Georg von Schonerer, who used anti-Semitism to become elected to the Reichstag in 1873, and Karl Lueger, who became mayor of Vienna in 1891. These two demagogues served as models for Adolf Hitler to use anti-Semitism to gain political power in Germany. They also served as models to current demagogues, who harness the anger of many economically insecure and underemployed white males in our society by blaming blacks, immigrants, Jews, Latinos, and women or to discredit more liberal politicians.

The factory owners in the nineteenth century also advanced the concept of individualism by feeling entitled to be concerned only about profits, but without a sense of civic responsibility or humanitarian concern for their workers' welfare. Because the factory working conditions were generally miserable and the work monotonous, men often sought stability and power at home. Robbed of a sense of mastery and achievement in their work, most men sustained their male identity and pride by exerting control over their wives and children. When one is degraded, looking down at and controlling another individual may be used to bolster a poor sense of self-esteem.

## PSYCHOLOGICAL ADAPTATION

Even more than in the past, Victorian men split off and used projective identification to displace aspects of themselves experienced as weak and powerless into women (Slipp 1993). Men could live vicariously through women, who contained and enacted these unacceptable aspects of men. Women were induced and then demeaned for being weak and dependent, thereby preserving and enhancing the personality of men. The "little woman" had to remain childlike and powerless to build her husband's male ego. Although men's identity and power were diminished in the workplace, in the home they were enhanced.

A symbiotic relationship was established between the genders, where men lived vicariously through women, and women gained their identity and self-esteem by identifying with and living vicariously through men. Women's role in the home remained the same, and they continued to be defined by their encompassing role function in the family. Women did not have a separate identity, needing to satisfy the needs of their husbands and children. To be otherwise was considered selfish. In exchange, women gained protection and respectability, though often not loving sex or intimacy.

The Industrial Revolution produced dramatic changes in the identity not only of men but also of women. A gender identity war gradually developed between the sexes, as women sought not to be constricted by men and to strengthen their identities as individuals. On the broadest level, this was made possible for women by technological and scientific advances in our society. The appliances produced by the Industrial Revolution, such as stoves, refrigerators, sewing machines, washing machines, mixers, irons, and so on, diminished household drudgery. Women did not need to spend their time making all the family's clothes and food, since they were inexpensively produced in factories. In addition, job opportunities for women opened up outside the home. Women and children were hired in factories and offices.

In communal societies women were chattel, with men having possession over their bodies, property, and even the children they bore. However, medical progress allowed women to gain more control over their own bodies. It provided better methods of birth control so that women did not have to repress their sexuality. There was also less need to have large families to compensate for the high death rate of infants. The birth process became safer and most childhood diseases were eradicated. Women did not need to be bound to the home for the family and society to survive.

Progress was slow, however, and most Victorian women were still deprived of an individual identity, and gained a sense of self only by identifying with and living vicariously through their husbands or children. Beginning in the eighteenth century, a small group of suffragist women fought to breach the rigid boundaries and constricted identities and roles prescribed by patriarchal society. They rebelled and sought to define themselves not in terms of function, but as whole human beings, capable of choice.

These early feminists rebelled against the restricted lifestyle that deprived women of the right to vote, custody of children, ownership of property, and an education.

As social constraints loosened, women fought to achieve the potential for greater freedom and power over their lives, no longer to be passive victims of society. During the nineteenth century, as families moved more and more from an agricultural to an industrial lifestyle in the city, the restraining influence of extended families was diminished. Although this allowed greater individual freedom for both sexes, the social dislocation reduced the solidarity of the family and its support network. The Industrial Revolution helped demolish the communal society that had previously existed.

## BREAKDOWN OF SOCIAL TIES

Just as had occurred under feudal lords, factory and mine owners felt entitled to exploit men, women, and children as dehumanized objects for their individual profit, but now even the vestige of civic responsibility for the welfare of their workers that existed during feudalism was lost. The protection that had been offered by an extended family and the community was diminished or gone. The loss of this safe holding environment was replaced by governmental laws and social legislation to better working conditions and to provide a safety net for the unemployed, sick, and aged. Labor unions formed to protect the workers by negotiating contracts through collective bargaining and by using the power of the group to call a strike or to stop production as leverage against the employer.

## Emancipation of Women
## from Social Constraints

During World War II the workforce in the United States also changed. It became necessary for women to work in defense and other industries, since men were away fighting. Just as it was hard after World War I to keep men down on the farm after they had seen Paris, it was difficult to keep women shut up in the kitchen once they had experienced a broader life. After the war, women were encouraged to give up their jobs to the returning veterans and to find fulfillment again in being housewives and mothers. This also suited industry, which was converting from the production of war material to domestic goods. Putting women back in their traditional role in the home created a market for household appliances and products.

The sexual revolution of the 1960s allowed women to start emancipating themselves from an inhibiting sexual lifestyle. It was the feminist movement, however, led by Betty Friedan (1963) in America, Simone de Beauvoir (1961) in France, and others that provided the group support that enabled women to feel entitled to emancipate themselves from a constricted, role-bound existence, which Friedan called the "feminine mystique." Liberated from the cultural gender stereotypes, women felt entitled to leave the kitchen and re-enter the workforce.

The resulting economic independence of women helped set in motion further challenges to the traditional gender roles that defined what was masculine and what was feminine. As more and more women felt empowered, they would not settle for a subordinate role in relation to men. They fought against male privilege and against being rigidly defined by a patriarchal society as only housewives and mothers, that is, the Victorian role functions of children, cooking, and church. They could pursue a separate individual identity, and not simply be used as objects to enhance male identity.

Women now, whether or not they call themselves feminists, feel entitled to *choose* a homemaker and/or career lifestyle and make their own life decisions. Some women do not wish to be considered feminists. A backlash against feminism has arisen because of some radical feminists who blame men as evil oppressors and view themselves as passive victims. However, radical feminists, who are anti-male, are only one small part of the feminist movement and the entire movement cannot be stereotyped and defined negatively this way. The feminist movement is varied and diverse, with many groups advocating better relations with men (Friedan 1981).

In the United States, most women now expect emotional and sexual satisfaction, and feel entitled to an equal partnership with men at home and in the workplace, to be fulfilled and to remain vital human beings. Unless trapped by dependency, physical violence, or economic insecurity, women are free to leave an unsatisfying, deadening, or abusive marriage. Leading a martyred life is no longer reinforced and rewarded as an ideal as it was in Victorian society.

The freedom of women to leave an unsatisfying marriage is a shock to many men, and has contributed to an increase in domestic violence against women. It is not the feminist movement that is to blame, but the difficulty that many men have in allowing women to be fully human and not to function only as a part-object, to compensate for men's threatened self-esteem and masculinity. Many men have been raised in traditional homes, where their model for male identification was a father who was privileged, powerful, and distant. These men now find it difficult to give up control, share power, and to be emotionally close. Often they are out of touch with their own feelings and are not accustomed to verbalizing their thoughts and feelings to resolve conflict, which has contributed to an increase in spousal abuse and violence. In a 1982 study (Goleman 1995) of men who murdered their wives or companions, the most important factor was their feeling rejected and unable to control their mate's actions.

## SOCIAL AND ECONOMIC CHANGES

On a broader social level, a polarization has occurred between communal and individualistic forms of society. Conservative movements have attempted to resist the transition to an individualistic form of society so as to maintain their power base and to retain the security of the communal form of society. A new form of imperialism has evolved, based not on economics but on ideology, with certain groups attempting to impose their beliefs on others. They neither restrict their values to their own group nor seek an accommodation with other groups, but feel justified in demeaning, obstructing, or even killing those who disagree.

The most recent social cause for the gender conflict is the changing economy. It is not simply that women have become stronger, but that many men have begun to feel weaker and insecure because of the sweeping changes in the workplace. The underlying reason is the financial insecurity and dislocation experienced by men as many American jobs have changed from múscle and sweat to computerized technology in industrial production; a change that has resulted in a mismatch of the skills required for this new industrial society, where advanced technical knowledge is required.

In many ways it is similar to the mismatch of skills that affected men over a hundred years ago during the Industrial Revolution. Just as men then wrecked the new factories out of the fear that they would be unemployed, men today are also threatened and feel powerless, since industry can produce more with fewer people. Fewer unskilled or semiskilled manual workers are needed because they have been replaced by robots. Even when some manual labor is needed, it often requires finer dexterity, at which women seem more adept.

In addition, many companies have moved their plants to third-world nations, where labor costs are much lower and where there are no unions or governmental regulations to protect workers and the environment. Striking can no longer be used by a union as a weapon, since the factory itself is gone and there are no strikebreakers for union workers to fight. The power of unions has been diminished as the number of members has been cut in half over the past twenty years. Transnational corporations have evolved to take advantage of monetary issues and cheaper labor and to deal with a competitive global economy and reduced profit margins.

Many of the companies that have remained in the United States are "downsizing," a euphemism for ruthlessly firing large numbers of their employees to run "mean and lean." Downsizing the workforce has become necessary for American companies to be able to compete with foreign companies in Asia and Europe. Cutting labor costs keeps the cost of production low, which is necessary to survive in the competitive world marketplace. Workers cannot demonize their bosses as they did during the Great Depression, since they realize their employers may also be helpless victims in the fierce competition of a global economy. Downsizing, however, has increased corporate profits and the value of stocks, which benefits the self-interest of top management and stockholders but penalizes the vast majority of employees.

Middle- and low-level management and clerical employees are also being fired, not only blue-collar workers. The result is a proletarianization of many middle-class men, who have to take lower-paying jobs. If the company is interested primarily in its bottom line of profit, and sees employees in dehumanized terms, employees may feel it's every man for himself. Individualism begets individualism. Loyalty to a company has almost been lost due to a lack of protection and harsher hiring and firing practices. There has been a decline in workers' expectations and an increase in cynicism, resentment, and distrust of authorities as a result.

An analysis of Census Bureau information for 1994 by Jared Bernstein and Lawrence Mishel of the Economic Policy Institute in Washington, D.C. (1995), noted that men's salaries had declined in almost all occupations. Men that were laid off lost around 20 percent when they were employed on new jobs. Although the lowest-paid 20 percent of women also earned less, the earnings of women managers and professionals rose over 2 percent. Most men feel powerless to deal with these larger economic issues in our society, with industry now driven by knowledge and robotics, downsizing, and exporting jobs out of the country. Many men do not have the skills that new industries require, and they feel angry that they have to settle for lower-paying jobs. Most men feel threatened by the competition of an increased pool of workers as women have entered the workforce. Thus many men object to women working, and may blame them for the fewer well-paying jobs that are available. They may not realize, however, that working wives may provide them with an economic buffer and provide the time and opportunity to learn skills for the new high-technology world.

## MEN AS THE VICTIMS OF SOCIETY

Threatened by a society in transition and by job insecurity, many men feel victimized and regress to a symbiotic survival pattern, with paranoid thinking and the search for an enemy to attack. (This is also an example of Bion's fight/ flight basic assumption group, which results when people feel helpless. Bion, however, focused more on unconscious shared fantasies, whereas my focus is on group survival even at the expense of individual autonomy.) This regressive way of dealing with frustration by scapegoating is similar to the events at the turn of the last century that gave rise to totalitarianism, the Holocaust, and World War II. The result is that many men, like their Victorian ancestors, personalize and scapegoat women, liberals, and other racial and religious groups. Many white middle-class men do this, since women and minorities have gained some privilege in the competition for jobs because of equal employment opportunity legislation, like the Civil Rights Act of 1964.

Men in the lower socioeconomic classes, blue-collar and unemployed men who were not affirmed economically and felt powerless, could previously bolster their male definition of themselves by feeling superior to women. This now becomes less possible as women are employed, especially when women are also hired to do physically strenuous or dangerous jobs. These types of jobs had been restricted to men and bolstered male identity. Not only can women not be put down by these men as inferior, but when women hold down these jobs it may be experienced as a direct attack on men's masculinity. To add to these men's sense of powerlessness, they also have felt displaced by illegal aliens and minorities who, they feel, are taking away their jobs. The real issue here, however, is the shrinkage in blue-collar jobs, due to the use of robotics, downsizing, and export of semiskilled work to third-world countries.

The greatest economic devastation has occurred among African-Americans, so that increasingly large pockets of unemployment and poverty have evolved. According to a recent U.S. Census Bureau report (1992), employed black men earn considerably less than white men. African-American children are nearly three times as likely as white children to live in poverty, and while 36 percent live with two parents, 54 percent live with their mothers. A frustrated and angry underclass of black and Hispanic men, who cannot find employment and feel alienated from society, has developed. The result has been increased conflict between the races, with polarization of blacks against whites. There has also been a backlash among black men against other minorities, such as Asians, and illegal aliens. This conflict extends into gender relations, with increased violence in the family, especially against women.

## CONFLICT BETWEEN
## SCIENCE AND SPIRITUALITY

Industry has as its primary goal achieving profits, but has not assumed sufficient humanitarian social responsibility for this new economic dislocation. This conflict has been true historically since the beginning of the Industrial Revolution. It is a continuation of the conflict between science, which emphasizes rational thinking and individualistic values, and religion, which highlights spiritual values and human relations. Lack of social responsibility is especially destructive now, since the family is less stable and the social support network of extended family, community, and religious affiliation is reduced or even lacking. If governmental social legislation for the poor is further reduced, greater polarization of society between the wealthy and the poor will occur. The government's war against poverty may become the war against the poor. The outcome will be a greater potential for the eruption of war between classes and races. The danger is that present-day demagogues may harness this helplessness, anger, alienation, and scapegoating to gain political power for themselves.

The frustration and powerlessness that people feel is made worse because they have greater expectations and feel entitled to happiness. Previously, expectations were lower and individuals were willing to accept unhappiness as part of life and to become resigned. They could compensate, however, even if they had an unsatisfying marital relationship, by obtaining support from an extended family or same-sexed peer group in the community. Men would go to bars or fraternal organizations to gain support from other men, while women often maintained relationships with their parents, women friends, and religious institutions. Since society now is less communal and more individualistic, this social support network has gradually eroded or disappeared.

Many women, however, have been able to establish friendships with other women, to form what can be considered a substitute extended-family network. This solidarity has enabled many women to exercise the empowerment obtained from the sexual and feminist revolutions. This current situation is more of a problem for men, who have been socialized to be independent and often have few intimate friends. As economic pressures increase, these men are more dependent on emotional support from their wives. Paradoxically, it is not the women but many white middle- and lower-class men, who had previously been privileged, who now feel persecuted and experience themselves as the passive victims of society.

Men's sense of powerlessness makes them more vulnerable either to demoralization and loss of hope in a better future or to regression. If regression occurs, men resort to a more primitive way of functioning, with splitting and paranoid thinking. This was found to contribute to an increase in violence against women. By victimizing another, one can achieve an illusion of power. In a 1985 survey of over six thousand American households by Richard Gelles, a sociologist at the University of Rhode Island (Goleman 1995), 90 percent of men who kill their wives have a history of abusing them. Gelles found ten factors that contributed to men being severely abusive to their wives, many of them economic. Men were more likely to be unemployed or to hold jobs making less than $15,000 a year, to be 18–30 years of age, to use drugs or alcohol, to have dropped out of high school, to have experienced their fathers hitting their mothers, to have lived in highly violent neighborhoods, to have been violent toward their children, to have not married or have been separated, and to have come from different religious or cultural backgrounds from their spouses. These men felt powerless, had low self-esteem, felt economically and sexually insecure, were impulsive, and used coercive physical violence to deal with conflict.

## LOSS OF SOCIAL RESTRAINTS

Because of societal changes, group values and norms have become more relative and less binding than they had been in the past, since survival is no longer dependent on close family ties. Thus the social restraints that defined and protected relationships have been weakened. For many people, individualism is more important than group identity. The anonymity of large-city life and universal education tend to diminish differences that existed between people. The freedom to assimilate into the mainstream and not to be identified with a minority group may open up more economic and social opportunities. As a result, there has been an increasing rate of intermarriage among various socioeconomic, racial, religious, and ethnic groups. Cultural differences within these marriages can create conflict, since misunderstandings can arise from misinterpretation or lack of knowledge of the other's cultural traditions and values.

In a society that has become less verbal, and where violence is idealized in movies and television, the chances of resolution of differences through dialogue are diminished. In addition, some families may reject those individuals that intermarry, creating alienation, pain, and further conflict. Extended family members may be concerned that the religious or ethnic communal values and traditions of one or both spouses may become so diluted that group identity will be lost, especially in their children. These are issues the therapist needs to be aware of and needs to help the couple resolve, since they compound problems in these marriages. One book that can help therapists become sensitive to ethnic issues is *Ethnicity and Family Therapy*, edited by Monica McGoldrick, John K. Pearce, and Joseph Giordano (1982).

## THE HISTORY OF ANARCHIC INDIVIDUALISM IN MODERN SOCIETY

The most notable revolt against established authority occurred during the Enlightenment of the eighteenth century. Voltaire, the most important of the philosophers, attacked the nobility, which oppressed people, and the church, which he felt constricted individual liberty. When Voltaire died, written on the funeral carriage were the words, "He gave the human mind a great impetus; he prepared us for freedom" (Durant 1927, p. 275). The Enlightenment philosophers provided the theoretical underpinnings for the American and French revolutions and the evolution of democracy. The growth of science and capitalism was also enhanced by this individualistic thinking. The death of religion was forecast, to be replaced by reason. The Enlightenment emphasized individualism, rationality, realism, and materialism, whereas the older communal culture stressed social constraints, morality, order, faith in established authority, and responsibility to others.

A further loss of faith in established patriarchal authority began around the turn of the last century. There was a general revolt of sons against their fathers (Schorske 1981), which resulted in marked changes in architecture, art, literature, music, philosophy, politics, and psychology. Even the philosophy of the Enlightenment fathers, which emphasized reason and science, was rejected by Schopenhauer and Nietzsche. Philosophy now stressed a further extension of individualism—inner will, power, and sexuality to provide men with vitality and creativity.

Nietzsche wrote that God was dead, and revolted against the paternal authority and "herd morality" of Judeo-Christian religion. He felt that to be a creator one needed to destroy old values. Drawing from the scientific discoveries of Charles Darwin, Nietzsche advocated a philosophy of individual empowerment, to create supermen in his "will to power." Walter Kaufman (1974) interprets the superman concept described by Nietzsche as meaning victory over himself and not others, thereby emancipating himself as an individual from a slave morality. But Nietzsche emphasized individual self-realization at the expense of civic responsibility and altruism, considering the latter a form of weakness.

After World War II, the existential movement embraced a nihilistic philosophy, which lost confidence in the truth of established paternal authority and its theories and looked only to immediate individual experiences. The current postmodern movement also considers that truth is relative, a metaphor, a narrative, shaped by individual subjectivity. Meaning is constructed through dialogue between people, and thus is intersubjective and relative. Some postmodern theorists even deny that there is anything like reality or universal truth. There are certain schools of family therapy that adhere to this philosophical stance and engage in mutual storytelling. They see all the patient's experiences as real, on a par with and equal to what most of the world considers reality. This may result in a folie à deux and in lack of differentiation of fantasy from reality.

Even though what society considers reality is not absolute and is only probable, it is closer to the truth, and adaptive in our society. Not all perceptions of reality are equal, and those generally accepted by society usually have greater pragmatic value. With the advancement of science and knowledge, our constructs are not permanent and absolute, but change over time anyway. An example of the misuse of postmodern relativism occurs when a therapist goes along with a patient's fantasy of sexual seduction and does not bother to find out if it is real. It is important to have an empathic connection with the patient, but the therapist also needs to serve as the voice of a more objective reality. This is described by the term *participant observation*. By not functioning this way, the therapist can reinforce a distortion of reality and subsequently open the door for a malpractice suit.

All these individualistic developments serve to weaken the respect for the therapist as a knowledgeable authority. More globally, when compliance to all authority is diminished, not only the family but the community too becomes destabilized. Here, individualism becomes anarchic and replaces responsibility to the family and society. Authority becomes the enemy.

## NEGATIVE CONSEQUENCES OF AN INDIVIDUALISTIC SOCIETY

Another problem has arisen in modern society as the authority structure is attacked by this extreme form of individualism. In communal society, older members were seen as wise and respected, since they passed on tradition. However, the rules and values of the groups that had enabled people to survive through communal life have lost a good deal of their former strength. Today, an urban society is more individualistic, often viewing authority as constricting or exploitative, and having the goal of individual self-expression and fulfillment. Often, the younger generation distrusts and rejects authority and does not feel that the past generation has anything to teach. At the worst extreme, there has been a breakdown of moral values and family stability, increased violence, and what some have called a "culture of narcissism" that is empty at its core, based on what one wants personally and not what may be socially responsible.

According to Jean Elshtain, Professor of Ethics at the University of Chicago (1994), the attitude of entitlement for individual rights, especially by men, has grown so much that it is all-pervasive. It is sought by conservatives, who advocate a free market as a basic human freedom. Liberals have advanced the pursuit of individual identity, which has politicized issues in private life, with each group feeling victimized by others. This has led to a polarization of group identities in America, such as men against women or whites against blacks, and vice versa, with a resultant loosening of civic ties that facilitate verbal discourse. The warring groups, whether based on gender, ethnicity, or religious identities, do not share common interests or engage in dialogue to resolve differences, resulting in what Elshtain calls the "end of conversation." Each feels victimized by the other and distrustful of the other's self-interest. Civil groups that transcend the closed boundaries of identity are needed to establish a common ground for verbal dialogue. Reiterating this concern, John Gay (1995) of Oxford University comments that if individual rights are considered absolute and unconditional, civic dialogue gives way to violence, as has occurred at abortion clinics in America. Then anarchy reigns.

## THE IMPACT OF THE MASS COMMUNICATION MEDIA

Many feel that the mass communication media—television, movies, and music—do not simply reflect modern society but also contribute to the current state of affairs, in which individualism and violence are idealized. Repeated exposure to violence in the mass communication media may desensitize many individuals, especially boys and men, and make violence more acceptable as a method of problem resolution. The alienation from the larger community, due to lack of economic opportunity and racial and ethnic prejudice, may make violence seem a suitable form of protest and ventilation of anger among the poor. In addition, the loss of respect for civil authority, which is not seen as a protective and concerned parental surrogate, has contributed to a search by some for personal power in crime and violence.

For a stable society, integration of individual and group identity is essential, as well as ongoing constructive dialogue (and not violence) to resolve differences and conflict. Neither the extremes of a symbiotic survival group pattern nor anarchic individualism are adaptive. Responsible relationships and individual freedom need to go hand in hand. These same goals are also crucial for the survival of the family. Asserting individual autonomy while preserving the safe holding environment of the family and community often present a problem for which couples seek help. These forms of relationships cannot be polarized, but must be integrated to achieve greater fulfillment of oneself and other family members.

Betty Friedan, in her book *The Second Stage* (1981), exhorted women not to band together as victims against men as their oppressors, but to achieve equality by working with men. In therapy, we can help clients learn that through verbal dialogue they can retain personal integrity while sustaining the support from relationships with significant others, the family, and the community.

# 2

# Power Conflicts in the Modern Middle-Class, Dual-Career Family

## MALE PRIVILEGE

The feminist movement and the civil-rights legislation of the '60s challenged the entitlement that society had given to men for power over women. This development is now coming to fruition as women seek equality with men at home and in the workplace. Men cannot simply impose their will in an authoritarian manner on women, since most women now are not economically dependent on their husbands. Opportunities for employment have opened up and provided women with economic independence, so that they need not be trapped and helpless in unhappy or abusive marriages. Out of choice and often out of economic necessity, the majority of American households now have both husband and wife as wage-earners. From 1972 to 1990 the number of traditional one-earner families dropped from 42.3 percent to 15.8 percent (Noble 1994).

In older traditional society, being the wage-earner served as the power base for the husband, and entitled him to certain role privileges and expectations. When a man came home from work after toiling all day as the breadwinner, he expected to be comforted and rewarded for his efforts. He wanted his wife to be selfless, to attentively cater to his needs, and to prevent the children from disturbing his peace. The traditional wife was expected to function as a good, nurturant mother, yet to be childlike and powerless. She was supposed to be the "little woman" who submitted to her husband's wishes. Childcare and household chores were strictly women's work, considered inferior or less important than man's work.

Men's primary identity and self-esteem rested on their occupations, which also was the case for women who lived vicariously through their husbands. Women's work was considered trivial, while men's work was meaningful and important. Men received money that enabled the family to survive, and the man could thereby fulfill his social role as the protector and breadwinner. Fulfilling this role expectation provided the man with the leverage that entitled him to dominate the family. For a man to put on an apron and help his wife with the dishes might make others question whether he was a real man, or even imply he was homosexual. For a woman to expect her husband to help at home or for her to be career oriented might result in others questioning whether she was suffering a masculinity complex or might even be a lesbian.

In modern dual-career families, since the man and woman are both working, they each have a power base and feel entitled to make demands of their spouses. The wife expects to be an equal partner, not simply a child/mother to her husband. She feels justified in expressing and expecting satisfaction of her emotional and sexual needs as well. Being a selfless martyr, submitting to her husband's will, is no longer socially admirable or rewarded, nor is it even a practical physical alternative when she is also working.

Since the wife shares the breadwinning role, she expects her  husband to share the wifely role. In the dual-career family, the roles of housekeeping, cooking, shopping, and childcare can no longer be the sole domain of women. Traditional role boundaries, which had previously been sharply defined by sex, are now blurred. Men are now expected to take an equal share of these responsibilities and to be a close and cooperative friend. The transition for men has been difficult, since in current society many men feel they should be the boss of the family, which had been the masculine role model learned from their fathers. Men have been trained to be competitive, to establish dominance hierarchies, but women do not want to be controlled in a dominant/submissive power relationship as they had been in Victorian society.

This transition creates the potential for considerable discord between the sexes. Many men feel conflicted about sharing responsibilities in the home with their wives. Performing household and childcare functions, which was considered feminine and inferior in their childhood, may represent a loss of status and power for many men. Considerable conflict around who does the shopping, housekeeping, and childcare arises. Recent surveys indicate that women still do most of these homemaking activities, even when they are employed. Often, men do not see these chores as part of their shared responsibility, but are happy to help out around the house. In this way these men maintain a superior position without losing status.

Many husbands do not see the equality desired by their wives as a true partnership. Instead, it is experienced as a threatening reversal of the power structure, with the wife becoming dominant. Since male identity for these men is based on a hierarchical power structure of dominance and submission, their sense of masculine identity is often threatened. They may feel they are wimps or momma's boys if they listen to their wives' wishes. They may feel that their sexual power as males is compromised if they do not dominate their wives generally in the home.

Men's need to maintain a dominant position has pre-oedipal, oedipal, sibling, and biological antecedents. Consciously or unconsciously, this fear of reversal of power may occur because men may resurrect childhood images of themselves as young boys under their mother's domination. Primitive anxiety about maternal engulfment or abandonment may also be revived. In the recent presidential election, this was reflected in the irrational fears of some conservative right-wing politicians that women who become feminists would kill their children and abandon their husbands to become witches and lesbians. In object relations terms, this is an example of regression to childhood fears and the use of the primitive defense mechanism of splitting of the preoedipal mother. The good nurturant mother might be transformed into the bad, destructive, and abandoning mother.

Men are also sensitive to power issues because of the oedipal conflict with the father. The father possesses the mother, toward whom the young boy has sexual feelings. Father is physically more powerful, and has a larger penis. For the boy to have sexual feelings toward the mother is threatening when the father is seen as restrictive and punitive. In traditional society fathers are not experienced by boys as nurturant and beneficent but as distant, strict, and enforcing discipline. Often mothers postpone punishment and assign this role to the father with the words, "Wait till your father comes home, and will he give it to you!"

The power structure in the traditional family was dominant/submissive. There were areas of dominance for each gender, with Mother having power over the household and children, but Father holding overall power. In certain instances, as in immigrant and poor families, when the father was not able to fulfill his role as provider he often would consider himself, and be considered by others, as a failure and surrender authority to his wife. Out of necessity the mother might take over leadership from a demoralized husband. The mother's power base as mother and housewife remained intact, which provided her with the confidence to take over the reins. In this case, the family power structure still remained hierarchical, with a dominant mother and a submissive father. Since there was generally no previous family model of equality, sharing is often equated by men with submission and total loss of power.

In relationship to one's siblings, there was also a pecking order and rivalry for positions of power. Usually the eldest sibling was entitled to a greater position of authority and responsibility. This was institutionalized in society, up to the Victorian era, as the eldest male inherited the family fortune. In addition, much of the external world is hierarchically organized, for example, the fields of education, sports, business, government, the military, religion, and others, so that cooperative sharing of power is not a general phenomenon in society.

## GENDER IDENTITY CONFLICTS

Currently, many men are experiencing role conflict about what it means to be a man. These perceptions also often remain polarized into extreme opposites. Is he supposed to be the soft and sensitive Mr. Mom, or the hard and

detached Mr. Macho? To preserve their marital relationships, men are called upon to function in a manner quite
different from their fathers, who were their original role
models for masculinity. Clearly not all fathers fit the
stereotyped male role, since there are individual differences. However, the stereotyped male gender role was
to be distant, silent, unemotional, and controlling. John
Wayne, Gary Cooper, or Clint Eastwood, who fit the
stereotype, might have been adaptive in the Wild West
when physical survival was threatened and quick action
necessary, but it is no longer a male model suitable for a
modern marriage. Women expect men to be more emotionally sensitive to them, in a cooperative and intimate
relationship. This may be a difficult task, since many
men have difficulty experiencing their own feelings and
communicating them, which is essential for an intimate
relationship.

In examining the preoedipal development of boys (from
birth to 4 years of age), we find that their first identification is with the mother, which forms the core of the ego.
Boys then need to gain distance from their mothers to
prevent engulfment, to establish firm boundaries, and to
achieve a masculine gender identity (Dinnerstein 1976,
Greenson 1968). In traditional society the mother was the
sole caretaker of children and invested with all the family power of this role. The father was not involved, being
identified with his role of breadwinner outside the family. Thus the preoedipal mother was seen by the infant as
all-powerful, making the process of separating from the
mother and achieving a male gender identity more difficult. To separate, the boy had to oppose and demean all
that was perceived as feminine, including the relationship
with the mother and any aspect of the self seen as like

her, in order to feel masculine. Dependency on the mother, crying, or emotionality were considered weaknesses and needed to be repressed. No boy wanted to be called a sissy or a momma's boy, even though young boys are still very dependent on their mothers.

In traditional society the father was not readily available as the boy distanced himself from the mother starting around 2 years of age. As the boy broke off his dependency on the mother, the father was not available emotionally to form an attachment. The result was an emotional trauma, resulting in the boy erecting narcissistic defenses of self-sufficiency to deal with this deprivation of nurturance and security from both parents.

Even though this early deprivation of dependency and the need to control the mother was self-initiated to establish male gender identity, it shaped the personalities of men and their relationships with both men and women in adult life. Many adult men have difficulty depending on and being intimate with men or women, and consequently have no close male or female friends. The need to diminish the power of the preoedipal mother continues to find expression in a need to control adult women. Because separation issues were traumatic in early childhood, a facade of not depending on anyone needed to be erected, and this extended into adult life. The lone cowboy who makes no attachments to women and is completely self-sufficient became the ideal. He was attached only to his horse and asserted his masculinity and power through physical action and his gun.

The issue of separation and distance from the mother was an ongoing problem in traditional society. Since the mother in Victorian society was denied an identity of her own, she often fulfilled her own frustrated personal ambitions by living vicariously through her sons. Thus, many mothers tried to maintain a close, binding relationship with their sons even into adult life to sustain their self-esteem and identity. From the son's perspective, the mother was experienced as invasive and not respecting individual boundaries. Thus many men had a continuing need to have a separate life of their own, making efforts to distance themselves from their intrusive mothers. Clear boundaries needed to be established between men and their mothers. This was a common pattern in Victorian culture, and separation from the mother was an ongoing problem from early infancy into adulthood.

As previously mentioned, Victorian women were not only controlled by men, but also became the repository of unacceptable aspects of men. This process began during early childhood. In order to separate from the mother around 2 to 3 years of age and establish a male gender identity, boys needed to split off from conscious awareness aspects of themselves felt to be unacceptable, such as dependency and weakness. These split-off aspects were put into girls and women through the defense of projective identification. This process was reinforced by cultural stereotypes, in which women were defined and saw themselves in society as emotional, dependent, and irrational, while men were unemotional, independent, and rational. Women were induced to contain and express these "weaknesses," for which they were demeaned. Men could then vicariously live through women. If women were weak, men could feel strong.

Due to the high infant mortality rate, women in Victorian society had large numbers of children, which contributed to most children's being emotionally deprived of maternal nurturance. The Victorian social structure, however, provided men with an opportunity to complete themselves later in adulthood though their wives. The wives not only contained men's unacceptable personality traits of dependency and emotionality that were split off and projected into them, but they were expected to function as nurturant good mothers to their husbands. Women were constricted in the psychological and social spheres due to this need for men to master their helplessness and their feeling of being controlled by the all-powerful preoedipal mother of early childhood. By considering women as childlike and weak, men could *reverse* the power relationships they had with their preoedipal mothers. The wife was now the child and the man the dominant parent. Men could expect women to be selflessly nurturant to help men master the traumatic loss of nurturance from their preoedipal mothers during childhood. The wife would now become the mother/child to fill her husband's emptiness. She would be not only the good nurturant mother but also the powerless child.

By fulfilling their roles of breadwinner and protector, men felt entitled to have their emotional and physical needs met first, above all others in the family. Wives had to comfort, feed, and support men's male egos. Being a mother to her children came second to being a wife/mother to her husband. This could mean getting the children out of the way so they did not disturb their father, or feeding father the best cuts of meat and other delicacies.

Even the Victorian dress of women emphasized the bosom and covered up her sexuality. Having a small waist, often achieved by tight corsets, almost cut her in half. She was the good, nurturant mother/breast but not the adult, sexual woman. The Victorian culture was constructed in such a way that it complemented and made up for the deprivation of maternal nurturance of men in their early childhood. During this era, men saw themselves as the protectors of women, which enhanced the sense of power and control that had been lacking during childhood. Although men projected their helplessness into women, women also experienced themselves as helpless and needy of men's protection. Women accepted this projected definition and colluded with the reversal of the mother/child role that had existed during early childhood. Women unconsciously contained this projective identification and traded off their own assertiveness and personal ambition to obtain this protection, so necessary in a society biased against women.

To be a marriageable commodity, a woman needed to be virginal, helpless, and to have repressed her sexuality as well. Sexuality was reserved for marriage, and was a part of the trade-off motivating a man to marry. After marriage, women could experience themselves also as part of the husband, and live vicariously through the husband's or son's achievement. Thus, while men lived through women to express unacceptable aspects of themselves, such as their helplessness, dependency, and emotionality, men also received nurturance that did not threaten their masculinity, as had occurred during childhood. In turn, women lived vicariously through men to achieve social status and to sustain their self-esteem.

Although gender roles were rigid, since each sex vicariously lived through the other, interpersonal boundaries were blurred. This made separation and divorce difficult, which was reinforced socially by considering divorce as shameful or sinful. Despite the low divorce rate, there was considerable conflict between the sexes. Women, being the weaker sex, needed to manipulate men, since they were blocked from personal assertiveness, anger, and self-fulfillment. Femininity was equated with manipulation, and was considered an inborn biological trait. Women tried to establish some control over their lives by using their feminine wiles. Women were taught not to be too smart or knowledgeable, to be charming and seductive, and to be weak and needy, which would attract a man.

Femininity was a learned social behavior taught by mothers to their young daughters, which provided some control over the helpless position women were placed into by society. In addition to repressing their assertiveness and needing to portray themselves as weak and needing protection, women also had to repress their sexuality, to be virginal, to be acceptable for marriage. Being strong or sexual would not attract a man's protection, and might well mean that men saw such a woman as a femme fatale. Overall, gender relationships were often not genuine, but were unequal, oppositional, and assumed a gamelike quality.

During the Victorian era, because of unresolved pre-oedipal and oedipal issues from childhood, men tended to split women into the good and bad mother. The result was the madonna/whore complex. Women were seen as good—selfless, motherly, and without sexual desires—or bad—selfish, aggressive viragos who were sexually vora-cious. Good women were not supposed to enjoy sex and had to be frigid and passive. Most men in Victorian soci-ety did not try to arouse their partners in foreplay. Thus the sexual problems of men, such as premature ejacula-tion, could be obscured. Many sexual problems between men and women were considered so much a part of the culture that they were not obvious. Many men had mistresses or used prostitutes with whom they could be sexual. The result was a high rate of venereal disease among Victorian men and many men had secret lives apart from their wives.

# 3

# The Effect on
# the Family
# of Male Unemployment

## DISORGANIZATION OF
## THE LOW-INCOME FAMILY

Disorganization in poor families often results from the inability of the male to fulfill his role as breadwinner. This inability may result from lack of opportunity or skills for employment or from racial, ethnic, or religious discrimination. Unfortunately, once this pattern has been established it often becomes a self-perpetuating vicious cycle, with negative reinforcement from society that militates against change. It is essential for the therapist to be aware of the cultural and psychological factors when working with this segment of society. However, not all families who are poor become disorganized, since many demonstrate remarkable coping skills and strengths and are able to function despite great adversity.

Most of the exploration of this segment of society occurred in the 1960s and early 1970s, since there was a general improvement in the economy during the 1980s. Oscar Lewis (1959, 1961, 1966) and Michael Harrington

(1962) have described the self-perpetuating subcultures arising out of poverty, which contain their own psychology, language, and world view. Defining poverty in its narrower or more concrete sense has largely determined the method of cure, namely, providing funds through welfare. Even if funds are provided without demeaning and dehumanizing bureaucratic practices, the process itself serves to perpetuate the family's passive dependency and alienation from greater society.

One method of counteracting the social disorganization resulting from poverty has been community action programs, which, like a therapeutic community in a hospital, encourage group cohesion, activity, and mastery. The community action programs were formulated to help develop indigenous leadership and community organization, as well as education and job training.

There have been studies of the effectiveness of community organization through self-help groups as early as the 1940s. Wittenberg (1948) found that in a slum area of New York City, as individuals felt better able to master their environment, they gained ego strength. Alexander Leighton (1965) was also able to facilitate social involvement and family integration of an economically deprived and disorganized white community in his Stirling County study. As occupational achievement was increased, there were also better educational aspirations, more community integration, and a significant decrease in psychiatric disorders. By now it is well documented through large-scale studies, such as those of Srole and colleagues (1961) and Hollingshead and Redlich (1958), that the poorest segment of society is afflicted with more psychiatric disorders and of a more severe nature than the middle and upper classes. Simply providing funds to cure poverty is not enough to counteract its devastating effects on individuals and families. Economic opportunity that incorporates men and women into society and gives them a sense of mastery and self-esteem is essential. As the old proverb goes, "It is better to teach people how to fish than to just give them fish." The government has become aware of the effects of poverty, and welfare reform is an important issue that is being addressed. It is essential to break the passive cycle of dependency and alienation, and to help poor individuals to become employed, active, and masterful, and to gain self-esteem.

The African-American family structure probably has suffered the most because of a long history of deliberate fragmentation of the family, harsh racial prejudice, and lack of economic opportunity. Lee Rainwater (1966) noted that since Emancipation, blacks were able to maintain complete nuclear families in rural areas just as well as similarly situated whites, since the male was able to fulfill his role function. The Puerto Rican family structure experiences stress due to the conflict between cultures. In Puerto Rico there is a traditional patriarchal family structure with extended family ties. However, in the United States there is a breakdown of primary group controls in favor of an isolated nuclear family, which is more individualistic and egalitarian. The resulting role strain between the spouses and between parents and children creates conflict. In addition to the change of power structure in the family, lack of economic opportunity for Puerto Rican males also has had a destructive effect.

Because of the social conditions that neither lead to a proud male image nor foster family solidarity, considerable frustration results. This may be turned against others, resulting in aggression and violence, usually within the same minority community, or the frustration may be turned against the self, resulting in self-hatred, poor self-esteem, apathy, work inhibition, and depression. The conflict in black identity has been studied and reported by Clark and Clark (1950, 1964), Johnson (1957), Milner (1953), and others. Rodman (1968) pointed out that a majority of ghetto residents identify and judge themselves by middle-class aspirations and values, while at the same time adhering to lower-class cultural values and attitudes. The large-scale study of Antonovsky and Lerner (1959) found that black children had a higher aspiration level than white children of the same income level. However, these aspirations were felt by the blacks to be disparate with actual expected levels of attainment. The result was a higher level of frustration and disillusionment, and a lower level of self-esteem.

Scanzoni (1967) found this same disparity between aspiration and expectation in white lower-class youths as well. The parents of lower-class youth inspired their children to achieve, but were unable to provide guidelines about realistic ways of achieving these goals, and were not adequate role models of success. Robert Merton (1957) noted that when middle-class aspirations and goals are internalized, but cannot be achieved through legitimate means in society, then the resultant "anomic" condition frequently produces deviancy and delinquency. This is especially true for young males, who may then resort to manipulation, cheating, seducing, or aggressively extracting through force what they want. One of the cases presented later will be that of a middle-class man, who as a child was expected to achieve, yet his father was absent and uninvolved and his mother was severely alcoholic, resulting in his becoming delinquent for a time.

Another adaptation for a man who experiences his environment as overwhelming is to become resigned, to lower his aspiration level, to become depressed and apathetic, and to live in fantasy. The result is a family structure in which there is withdrawal of emotional involvement with each other. This is described by Srole and colleagues (1961) and Langner and Michael (1963) in the New York Midtown Studies, and by Clark's (1950) study of black youth in Harlem, as well as the rural poor white community of the Stirling County study by Leighton (1959). All these studies found a pervasive sense of powerlessness, apathy, depression, hostility, cynicism, distrust of others, and intolerance for ambiguity or change. The Stirling group, which was white, was like many black and Hispanic poor groups, suffering from poor school performance with a high dropout rate, high incidence of broken homes, avoidance of work, lack of future planning, and a high prevalence of alcoholism and psychiatric disorders.

Family structure appears to differ more between different income levels than between racial groups, according to Herzog (1966). The inability of the adult male to function as breadwinner lowers his self-esteem, with the male becoming demoralized and considering himself a failure. This strips the male in traditional families of his entitlement to a dominant role (Komarovsky 1940). Marriage for the woman represents only subjugation to male authority without compensatory economic security, thus the woman may take over leadership in poor families. For the male, marriage means responsibility that is hard to meet and the prospect of humiliation. Thus both sexes may protect themselves by avoiding commitment to a permanent marital relationship. Rainwater (1966) notes that in the black ghetto culture, the female role model emphasizes self-sufficiency, which defends her against depending on the male. She is more secure when she takes over the leadership of the family and excludes the male into a peripheral position without authority. The black woman may be better able to find employment or go on welfare to survive. Rainwater noted conjugal role segregation, with husband and wife pursuing their separate interests. Neither expects his or her own needs to be fulfilled or feels able to fulfill those of the other. Usually there is pervasive segregation of the sexes, with males finding support in the street culture or in bars and clubs.

The woman's distrust of men's ability to fulfill their responsibilities hinders her also from entering into a permanent marital relationship. As a mother, she can express and gain affection from her children, without the risk of disappointment. The daughters may form an anti-male coalition with their mothers, and may have difficulty separating to establish a permanent relationship with a male. The Biebers' study (1968) showed this to be the case, with unwed mothers resistant to their daughters getting married despite such opportunities. The result tended to be a continuing cycle of unwed mothers and a matriarchal power structure.

For the male, social recognition can be achieved by recounting his sexual exploits to his same-sexed peer group. This external validation is an effort to compensate for the poor self-image as a male acquired from his experiences in his family, school, and society. Pettigrew (1964), Burton and Whiting (1961), and Kardiner and Ovesey (1951) reported on the black male's need to show exaggerated masculine behavior to defend against his insecure male identity. With Hispanic groups, there is an institutionalized, masculine-protest syndrome termed *machismo*, defining behavior that proves one's masculinity to oneself and others. This same finding was noted in poor white groups, where the family and society do not affirm masculinity. In England, for example, Spinley (1953) reported that the young white slum males had a predominantly feminine identification because their mothers possessed the power in the family, with fathers being unemployed, weak, or absent. These males showed marked insecurity about masculinity, feelings of inferiority, and tended to be overly aggressive and narcissistic to compensate. A matriarchal family power structure seems to be common in all industrial societies when the male cannot fulfill his role as breadwinner, regardless of race or ethnicity.

## THERAPEUTIC PROBLEMS WITH THE POOR

Unless the therapist is aware of the diverse values, expectations of treatment, language, and cultural patterns, he or she may have difficulty understanding certain behavior and may experience difficulty in establishing an empathic therapeutic relationship. The therapist needs to appreciate the *adaptive* significance of and accept those values that are part of the poor family's cultural patterns, as well as deal with psychopathology. The therapist needs to help the family modify those values that seem to perpetuate their social disorganization and stifle personal growth and change. To facilitate adaptation into the work world, the therapist needs to help males control their impulsivity, learn to delay gratification, plan ahead, and expand their horizons of opportunity through further education and training. The family can also learn to function as a cohesive group and provide a safe holding environ-

ment and mutual support to take advantage of job opportunities as they occur.

One of the first problems in treating poor individuals
and families is lateness or skipped appointments. If the
therapist handles this solely as resistance, or becomes
hostile, the man or family will probably drop out of treatment. Although it may be resistance, many poor individuals live in a chronic state of chaos and feel out of control
and unable to plan ahead. There may be a pervasive sense
of apathy or hopelessness, resulting in less value or importance placed on being on time for an appointment. In
addition, many poor patients do not take appointment
times seriously, since they often go to clinics and are kept
waiting long hours before being seen. Thus it is important
for the therapist to tell the patient or family that this is a
special time for them, and they will not be kept waiting.
The therapist needs to constantly reach out, telephone
when poor patients do not come in, and be willing to be
flexible when they are late without taking it as a personal
offense.

Many poor patients and families are suspicious of the
middle-class therapist, since he or she may be seen as an
extension of the impersonal social power structure or as
representing the authority of the entire clinic or hospital.
Past frustrations with doctors, social workers, psycholo-
gists, and other health professionals or even the hospital
or society as a whole may be displaced onto the middle-
class therapist. Thus, it is important to be patient and to
slowly pursue the development of a trusting relationship.
Some patients may submit to the authority of the therapist, but in turn demand an immediate, magical cure. If
this does not occur rapidly they may feel they are getting
second-class treatment or that the therapist is no good.

They may also feel that emotional problems can be cured by a pill or diet, while others may feel problems are due to a curse and can be cured by a spiritualist. To correct these assumptions the patient's ideas concerning mental illness, their expectations and goals, and the process of treatment need to be explained. In this way a workable therapeutic contract can be established.

It is important to start treatment with a patient or family where they are psychologically. Many patients experience their problems as outside themselves or due to concrete circumstances. Indeed, these outside circumstances often need to be dealt with before more subtle emotional factors can be approached. Thus, helping the patient at their level is important in order to make a therapeutic connection. Only later can their problems be redefined in another way. Emotional support, environmental manipulation, medication, or concrete suggestions may reduce symptoms and increase chances that the patient will trust the therapist and become engaged in further treatment.

To counteract the suspicion that may exist, the therapist needs to present himself or herself openly and honestly, sincerely concerned about the patient's problems. The therapist needs to show warmth and empathy, so as to enhance the patient's self-esteem. To facilitate engagement, the therapist needs to be more active and supportive, to reach out, to provide information, to elucidate and teach, and to offer concrete advice when indicated. Establishing a degree of rapport and intimacy fairly early in treatment is not always possible, but when it occurs it helps engage the patient and ensures continuation in therapy. On the other hand, while gratifying dependency needs, the therapist has to move patients in the direction of gradually assuming responsibility for themselves and achieving mastery. The guidance that the therapist can offer as a result of professional training has to mesh with the needs and expectations of the patient to provide a sensitive interchange.

In middle-class individuals, language is generally used in an instrumental fashion, to convey feelings and messages that will be received and responded to appropriately. Language is used not only as an expressive medium, but to convey meaningful content and to facilitate dialogue in problem solving. In lower-socioeconomic individuals, however, Bernstein (1962) noted that the language code was restricted, and experiences were perceived in a global, diffuse, nonanalytic manner. This was especially true for poor males, which resulted in experience not being differentiated or meaningful and tended to interfere with remembering, subsequent reporting, and learning. Minuchin (1964) noted that in lower-class families containing a delinquent, the verbal content of a message was frequently less significant than its command aspect, which defined power relationships. Scheflen (1963, 1964) found that nonverbal communication not only conveyed affect in all families but also served to regulate and control group interaction. Thus the therapist must be sensitive to nonverbal communication, and bring it up verbally for discussion. For example, a man may raise an eyebrow, and the therapist may note this and wonder if he is expressing how he feels, perhaps surprise or disapproval. Therapy helps the patient learn to identify and verbally express his feelings and thoughts more openly, and thereby to differentiate experiences. The therapist can help the patient recognize not only possibly negative feelings, but also positive concern, which he may have previously felt to be unmanly and unacceptable to express.

After a therapeutic alliance has been established, in which the patient can trust the therapist, a more active interpretive approach may be possible. The therapist can verbalize the sequence of verbal and nonverbal behavior so that interactive connections and patterns of behavior can be highlighted. In this way the therapist can help the patient become sensitive to cause-and-effect relationships. The patient can learn how he affects others, how they may experience him, and how their responses affect him. By becoming more aware of the impact he has on others, he may gain more control over how others respond to him. He can anticipate an outcome and can learn to plan ahead.

In working with poor families, focusing on the here and now instead of on memories of the past is often more helpful. However, at certain points in the treatment, insightful interpretations connecting the past with the present can be brought up. This helps the patient understand how current patterns of relationships may be repeated due to expectations and experiences from the past. In couples and family therapy, the therapist serves as a model to enable family members to reveal themselves more openly and honestly, and to establish a meaningful verbal dialogue. Having a heterosexual co-therapy team was also found to be helpful, in view of the distrust of the opposite sex and the segregation of the sexes in poor families. Each marital partner was able to form an alliance with the same-sexed therapist, yet observe how the male and female therapists cooperated and worked together.

At times, one family member who has more education or has had previous therapy can serve to bridge the cultural gap between the therapist and the other family members. At times, children serve this function, or may even reveal family secrets. As the family members' fears, frustrations, and resentments are brought to the surface, discussed, and worked through productively, expressing their feelings becomes more acceptable and less frightening. As each family member becomes more aware of the other as a human being with his or her own needs and limitations, a greater empathy and understanding can evolve between spouses and family members. Also, hopefully, as social opportunities for training and employment occur and there is a lessening of racial, ethnic, and religious bias, the vicious cycle of poverty, family and social disorganization, and psychopathology can be broken.

# 4

# Iron John,
# Iron Hans, Iron Cross

## HISTORICAL PERSPECTIVE

Although there are inborn biological factors, male gender identity is largely shaped by the culture and thus in need of continued external validation. From ancient times up to preindustrial society, masculine identity could be validated in several ways. In primitive, communal, warrior societies there were rites of passage that facilitated boys' acceptance into the community of men as hunters and fighters. In agricultural societies and small towns prior to the Industrial Revolution, fathers taught their sons skills that would enable them to run a farm or join a trade guild.

After the Industrial Revolution, the father's workplace was more often a factory or a business outside the home. These fathers no longer imparted useful knowledge about agriculture or technical trades to their sons. The father was less involved during childhood in helping his young son reach manhood, and the responsibility for childrearing rested solely on the mother.

## LACK OF FATHER'S
## INVOLVEMENT IN CHILDREARING

The lack of the father's presence and involvement with his sons became greater after World War II in the United States. Many families moved to housing in the suburbs, so that more time was spent by the father commuting back and forth to work in the city. The absence of the father as an involved and respected idealized figure was the theme of the book and movie *Rebel Without a Cause*. The sons needed to prove they were not "chicken" (unmanly) by performing life-threatening feats. The cause for rebellion was the lack of strong input from a father with whom to identify. The validation of a boy's masculinity often depended during adolescence on social success with one's peers, predatory sexual conquests of women, athletic prowess, or, especially among the economically disadvantaged, criminal behavior.

In the middle class, a boy might not have a great deal of nurturance and attention from his father, but he could identify with his father's self-measures of manhood, namely, success at work, material possessions, and social prestige. Thorstein Veblen (1899) described how, in the United States, keeping up with the Jones' materially, through conspicuous consumption, validated one's middle-class status. In America, where the Constitution states that all men were created equal, *achieved* status was significant, measured by the power derived from material possessions. Previously, in Europe, status was *ascribed*; social position depended on the family in which you were born, whether noble or commoner. With the rise of the middle class to power and the decline of the nobility, European social position has become like the American.

The middle-class male in modern America often feels pressured to continually prove himself materially as a successful breadwinner. His need to obsessively work long hours perpetuates his absence from the home and interferes with his ability to function as a father to his children. He often is proud that his wife does not need to work, further proof that he is a successful provider, a real man.

## PSYCHOLOGICAL FACTORS

A man's failure in work, sexually, or even socially often gave rise to fears that others would question his masculinity. Feeling powerless to fulfill the masculine work role was associated with loss of status and self-esteem, with feeling emasculated, and at times with fears of being homosexual. This is particularly a problem now with poor youths, especially those in racial or ethnic ghettos, who may have been raised without a father, who are alienated from society, and who feel hopeless and helpless about finding a job to feel powerful as a man.

Clearly the fear of becoming homosexual when there is a loss or absence of power is a misconception, since sexual orientation is different from gender identity. In homosexual sexual orientation, the individual has fantasies, often from an early age, involving sexual attraction to the same sex. The fear of becoming homosexual is a result of damage to one's gender identity, to the sense of masculinity, and of not feeling strong. It is a fear that if one is not a man, one is a woman. Indeed, most homosexually oriented men have intact male gender identity, but ignorance about differentiating the two is common in our culture. It is a major cause for homophobia, gay bashing, and

the need to prove one's masculinity through physical violence or crime.

The importance of the father in the lives of his children
also was not stressed in psychoanalytic theory, except
during the oedipal period from 4 to 6 years of age. In traditional society, it was the mother who was held responsible and to blame if anything went wrong. Since their
husbands were absent a good deal of the time and the role
of mother was their main source of power, identity, and
self-esteem, some mothers found it difficult to give up their
power over their children as they grew up. This problem
was compounded by the absence and lack of attachment
of fathers to their children and family, since the father's
priority was to work and prove his manhood by being a
good provider. Thus, as mentioned earlier, conflicts in
separation from the mother by boys were often not limited to the preoedipal period but continued through childhood and into adulthood.


## THE MYTHOPOETIC MEN'S MOVEMENT

Out of the crisis in male gender identity in our society,
Robert Bly became the guru of the "mythopoetic" men's
movement. This occurred after his television interview by
Bill Moyers in 1990, and his book *Iron John* (1990) was
on *The New York Times* hardcover best-seller list for sixty-
two weeks. According to Jill Johnston (1992), who also
interviewed Robert Bly, the book is autobiographical. Bly
overidentified with and felt bound to a damaged mother,
and was alienated from his alcoholic father, who was closer
to Bly's older brother. Bly blamed his mother for allowing herself to be victimized by her husband. Bly identi-

fied with her victimization, stating she was "locked in by this ogre in his castle" (Johnston 1992, p. 29). Johnston found that Bly did not escape his mother's feminine influence until he was 46 years of age, at which time his older brother died. He then acknowledged his father in his poetry, and opened himself up to identifying with his father and his masculinity. Years later Bly visited his sick father, and was able to grieve and resolve his anger for feeling rejected. He became aware that the opening to men's feelings is grief about their fathers. Bly's success probably came from his touching on unresolved issues for many men, "father hunger," and the crisis of masculine identity since the feminist revolution.

In response to men not having bonded with their fathers during their childhood, Bly's simplistic solution is to reinstitute the type of initiation ritual found in primitive warrior societies that validated a male's passage from childhood into manhood. In these rituals, women are excluded and devalued. Bly assumes the ritual will enable men to get in touch with the "wild man" and the warrior inside. He states that young males require an older male mentor (as he himself needed his father) in order to be emancipated from the powerful possessive mother. Men need tender and close relationships with men, which he terms "male mothering" (Johnston 1992, p. 31).

Bly uses the myth of Iron John, which is a fairy tale written by the Grimm brothers of Germany in the nineteenth century, originally called "Iron Hans." Iron John was a hairy wild man captured from under a pond in a forest and locked up in a cage in a castle. The king of the castle gave the key to Iron John's cage to his queen, who was thus symbolically given responsibility for her son's masculine development. One day the boy's golden ball rolled into the cage, and in exchange for returning it Iron John demanded his freedom. The son stole the key from under his mother's pillow and set Iron John free. Fearing punishment, the son returned to the pond in the forest with the wild man. After a series of adventures as a lowly cook and gardener in another king's castle, the boy enlisted Iron John's help to defeat an invading enemy. After winning a contest, the boy married the other king's daughter and lived happily ever after.

Bly stereotypes all mothers as powerful and possessive, and believes that a boy needs to steal the key (symbolic of masculine power) away from her to become a man (symbolized by Iron John). Bly seems unaware that he takes for granted the cultural context of this myth, especially the rigid gender role assignment under patriarchy that brings about this drama. Originally, the King/father handed over the childrearing responsibility to his wife and was uninvolved with his son. The mother was invested by the father with socializing her son (to contain the wild man in him).

What Bly describes is a traditional patriarchal family (like his own), in which a woman was trapped in the home and solely responsible for childrearing. Childrearing thus was the woman's primary source of power and self-esteem, which could make her unwilling to give it up, and might result in possessiveness over her children. Denied an ability to define herself and deprived of an equal and nurturing relationship with a husband, who was attached to his work, a woman often attempted to perpetuate her mother role. Being denied opportunity herself, she needed to feed her self-esteem by living vicariously through her son's achievements. This traditional family constellation tended to interfere with the process of separation (for children of both sexes) and the establishment of ego boundaries, and also deprived the boy of a nurturant, involved relationship with his father.

Bly uses stereotyping to describe all mothers as evil and emasculating, needing to be deceived by their sons to achieve independence and masculine power. This not only does not describe the major form of family constellation that exists today in the United States, where both parents work, but, worst of all, it continues the polarization of the sexes and the paranoid bias against women. Bly's prescription to prevent being victimized is for men to band together against women, who are devalued, blamed, and seen as villains.

Bly does not understand the cultural victimization of women or the father's responsibility in putting his work ahead of the family. In traditional families the weaker attachment of the father to his wife and children contributes to the high divorce rate and the large number of "deadbeat dads." The bottom line is that Bly's solution is regressive, encourages acting out against women as scapegoats, and increases the gender identity wars by blaming the mother.

Another scenario is possible however, and preferable, as described by Dorothy Dinnerstein (1976) and experimentally validated in the longitudinal study at Yale Child Study Center by Kyle Pruett (Salk 1990). Both the father and mother remain involved in childrearing, and both parents have an opportunity for self-fulfillment in their careers. The Yale Study found that children of both sexes raised this way seem to have more complete personality development without any negative effect on their gender identity. At 10 years of age, both boys and girls enjoyed nurturing babies and were also interested in work activities. This is adaptive to the middle-class family life these children will live as adults. Since the traditional family is now a minority, and families in which both parents work are in the majority in the United States, both parents need to share household and childrearing responsibilities. Thus gender roles are becoming less rigid and more cooperative and friendly.

If fathers share in childrearing, there is a greater potential for stronger attachment to their children and family. As a spinoff, this might diminish the increasing divorce rate, and even if divorce occurs, the fathers are less likely to disappear and refuse to pay child support. In addition, during the preoedipal period, the child experiences both parents as powerful. This dilutes the boy's perception of the mother as the evil, all-powerful witch who will trap him in a cage and eat him up, like the fairy tale of Hansel and Gretel. Thus the boy would not need to have his father help him emancipate himself from a close-binding and controlling mother. As the mother is not enslaved herself by a constricted gender role, she would not need to be intrusive and possessive to protect her sole source of power and identity. She would possess other keys to power in her life. As Jill Johnston (1992, p. 29) states, "If the mother doesn't stay home, the boy will have no good emotional reason for being pried away. There would be no initiation story."

## THE MACHO MYSTIQUE

Bly's solution clearly seems to represent a backlash against feminism. It perpetuates patriarchy, accentuates the war between the sexes, and does not provide an opportunity for conflict resolution through dialogue. Even in the tale of Iron John, the boy needs to prove his masculinity through winning a war and a contest and is awarded the princess by the other king. The boy does not marry the princess after achieving an intimate and loving relationship with her, into which they enter out of their own free will. The princess is not a person but an object, a trophy, that serves to prove the boy's masculinity.

Bly's solution for men is to regress to the puberty rituals of primitive warrior societies, in which sexual roles were sharply demarcated to ensure group survival. Boys learned to endure pain and frightening situations by suppressing their feelings and remaining focused on a task. These primitive societies blurred ego boundaries, with individuality harshly suppressed and group-mindedness reinforced, which was essential for hunting and war. Bly's wish to reinstate the patriarchal, macho mystique that was adaptive to primitive warrior societies is not adaptive to modern society. This macho mystique is exclusionary and hostile to women, and only produces warriors who will fight women and other men.

We now live in another type of society, which is attempting to diminish physical violence and increase communication. Primitive rituals no longer have any adaptive social function. We don't have to hunt and kill wild animals for our food or defend ourselves against hostile tribes. In modern society we need less violence, not more wild men who defend against their fear of not being masculine by a macho mystique. We need more mature adults capable of cooperation and dialogue.

As therapy to restore manhood, Bly recommends a weekend retreat, during which men beat drums, chant, dance, roar, recite poems and myths, and sit in a sweat lodge to bond with other men. This ritual seems a form of play, which mimics and is felt by many Native Americans to be disrespectful of the real religious meaning. The weekend ritual does not have the serious life-and-death consequences of preparation for survival that it had in those societies. It is a quick fix, based largely on activity that gives the illusion or fantasy of achieving manhood quickly. It is like the encounter movement of the 1960s, which promised instant intimacy without processing and working out the problems carefully through long-term verbal therapy. Bly gives lip service to therapy by encouraging men to relate stories of grief and loss, especially about their fathers, so as to get in touch with their inner "wild man." It does not, however, address the deep, emotionally laden, underlying issues that require longer psychotherapy for enduring personality change. In addition, it does not address the broader social issues, the need to make work no longer the responsibility solely of men and to encourage men's greater involvement with their children and wives. Only in this way can there be a cessation of "father hunger" through subsequent generations and a reduction in the divorce rate.

## STONE AGE SOCIETIES

From a scientific standpoint we can get a glimpse of ancient Stone Age societies, which still exist in New Guinea (Lidz and Lidz 1988, Malinowski 1929). Here women are assigned primary responsibility for childrearing up until puberty. The male child is then taken away and symbolically reborn through men. This rebirth is accomplished by an initiation ritual, which often involves physical abuse, mutilation, or repeated homosexual inseminations to get rid of the mother's influence and to create solidarity with the men. The boy must not be like his mother, and must renounce anything considered feminine. The underlying reason for the ritual is considered by many investigators to reflect men's fear and envy of the woman's magical power of creating and nurturing life, of womb envy and breast envy.

The culturally adaptive purpose of the ritual was to help the men of the tribe form a closely knit community for hunting, protection from animals and nature, or war with other tribes. Women were associated with nature, menstruating each month like the new moon, and birth was mysteriously connected with reincarnation of the dead. Women were the feared other, who had to be controlled as a denial of human vulnerability. This created a paranoid polarization of "us against them." Controlling women would control nature and death, which is an example of using magical thinking to strive for mastery.

In Bly's weekend retreats a revival of the macho mystique and a regression to patriarchy, misogyny, and idealization of the phallocentric male animal seems a regression to the Stone Age. This type of adaptation is also similar to the cults of manhood in Germany, which evolved from the philosophy of Nietzsche, and which were adopted by the Nazis. The "wild man" is a reincarnation of the pre-Christian blond beast and the superman that Nietzsche wrote about and that the Nazis misused to elevate themselves, to dehumanize others, and to create a warlike society.

## WAR OR PEACE

Group solidarity, suppression of individual identity, repression of emotions, and dehumanization of the enemy were used socially to get soldiers to fight wars. Since World War I, the introduction of airplanes, tanks, machine guns, chemical warfare, and long-range artillery has made warfare more devastating, involving also women and children civilians. Since World War II, artillery and aerial bombing have even been replaced by long-range intercontinental atomic missiles capable of vast destruction. As warfare has become more devastating and impersonal, the personality traits of repression of emotionality, detachment from human involvement, and the paranoia of seeing other groups as bad that were essential for tribal or national security are no longer adaptive. The increased ability to destroy vast numbers of people with nuclear weapons, as if one were playing a videogame against dehumanized others, becomes the greatest threat to all life on our planet. Paradoxically, this immense power to destroy all life on earth hopefully can provide the basis for universal cooperation instead of deadly competition in war. The alternative is unthinkable.

The essence of all religions—accepting one's own humanness and that of others—becomes a necessity in a global village. Religion and science each can contribute to responsible universal cooperation. Hopefully, as we become more civilized and learn to live together in a global world, gender, ethnic, religious, racial, and national differences can coexist without warfare. Restoring a patriarchal macho mystique with its exclusionary and regressive aspects of seeing women and others as bad and needing to be tricked, dominated, or defeated only increases the danger of nuclear holocaust and terrible disaster for all humanity.

Even on a smaller scale, in our own cities, releasing the "wild man" and the "warrior" is no solution to the increased crime and violence in our country. Youthful gangs already have initiation rituals in order to prove their masculinity. They embrace the macho mystique to feel power-ful, and idealize violence against others. Many of these gang members come from families without a father, who is physically absent, emotionally uninvolved, or abusive, and with mothers who are struggling to survive and un-able to parent and control their children. Boys grow up with diminished family attachment, internal controls, and responsibility, leading to a lack of care about what they do to others. These youths also feel emasculated and alien-ated from society because of the lack of economic oppor-tunity to fulfill the masculine role of breadwinner. Their male identity does not come from a caring father but from peer groups and the mass communication media, where macho characters are glamorized and violence is the model for resolving conflict.

An article by Don Terry in the September 3, 1994, edi-tion of *The New York Times* on teenage gang slayings con-tained the following paragraph: "Every day this week, it seems, the boy's story has provided a look into a world that is often left to suffer on its own. It is a slice of America where children become warriors, grown men give the or-ders and make the money, and the street gang is family, employer, and executioner" (p. 6).

If a man cannot get a job, he will avoid marriage be-cause he cannot meet its responsibilities. Ordinarily, many women are willing to trade a degree of their independence for economic and emotional protection by a man. Clearly, poor women do not get economic protection or emotional security from marriage and thus avoid this commitment. Most sociological studies indicate that males on the low-est economic scale tend to be most authoritarian, domi-nating, and even abusive to compensate for a manhood diminished by not being able to be a provider.

Thus, many socioeconomically poor women may prefer to go on welfare and keep men as sexual objects, without authority and peripheral to the family. Among some Puerto Rican women in New York City there is a saying, "I am living with Wilfredo," indicating that welfare is the provider. The answer to this situation is to provide economic opportunity for disadvantaged men, which will enhance self-respect, diminish hostility, and reduce alienation from greater society. Sociological studies conducted in Nova Scotia by Alexander Leighton (1965) and in England by Spinley (1953) indicate that providing economic opportunity diminishes disruption of families, alcoholism, and emotional disturbances.

A sense of community involvement can also be fostered through social and religious organizations. These civic institutions can facilitate respectful dialogue between various groups to help humanize others, diminish racial, ethnic, religious, and gender bias, and help to resolve issues verbally. Efforts to stabilize family life through parenting classes, social services, and child-care facilities are needed. For unmarried mothers with children, day classes can be established to increase parenting, homemaking, and occupational skills. In addition, premarital, marital, and family counseling and group therapy is useful in changing attitudes toward the opposite sex and a negative world view.

Other measures can consist of involving fathers in the birth process and in childrearing, so that the attachments to their children and family would be enhanced. The mass communication media can assume responsibility for helping to reestablish intimate human relations instead of greedily exploiting violence and sex for profit. This would not be an infringement on the First Amendment but a contribution to social responsibility. The media can help redefine masculinity in society away from narcissistic isolation and violence and toward human involvement. Bly's solution of acting out against women as the enemy or beating drums and crying about absent fathers will not help. Integration and not polarization of our biological urges with social responsibility is the answer for men to become civilized, caring human beings. Individual problems and differences between the sexes need to be resolved through better communication, mutual respect, and negotiation and not through isolation, physical force, abandonment, or drugs. This is where the therapist, using verbal communication to resolve conflict, serves as a model for society as a whole.

# 5

# The Theory and Practice
# of Therapy with Men

## HISTORICAL BACKGROUND
## OF GENDER THEORY

The major problem with Robert Bly's work is that he re-
lies on Carl Jung's (1959) speculation that there are certain biologically inborn archetypes, which Jung termed
*animus* and *anima*. These Jungian archetypes posit that
there are fixed masculine and feminine natures, which are
genetically endowed, born into each individual. This biological determinism is seen as unchangeable, and it denies
the importance of cultural stereotypes learned during
childhood and reinforced during adulthood.

Jung's constructs were derived from Greek and Chinese
philosophy, Charles Darwin's theory of evolution, and
probably the idea that everyone was born with bisexual
elements, as formulated by Sigmund Freud's friend,
Wilhelm Fliess. Fliess (P. Gay 1988) felt that varying
degrees of bisexuality existed, with feminine men choos-
ing masculine women to integrate their bisexuality.

There is an interesting story about the transmission of
Fliess's idea to others. Fliess had informed Freud about
his hypothesis of universal bisexuality, which Freud revealed to one of his patients, Hermann Swoboda. Swoboda
in turn told it to Otto Weininger, who wrote a popular book
about this in 1903 called *Sex and Character*. Weininger
stated that the inborn masculine element was responsible
for rationality, creativity, order, and positive achievements, while the feminine element was sexual, irrational,
emotional, chaotic, and destructive. Jung, who was influenced by this thinking, also speculated that the inborn
masculine component (animus) was associated with reason, while the inborn feminine part (anima) was related
to emotionality. He believed that these two components
then sought integration in the individual and also influenced the choice of a mate. Jung was not aware that these
components were not inborn but were primarily learned
gender stereotypes, which are transmitted from the culture through the family to the child.

Although there are biological potentials in each gender,
most of gender identity is learned during childhood. It
is the culture that defines men as rational and women
as emotional. Clearly, women and men are both rational
and emotional. It is mainly the socialization process that
polarizes these elements and influences which aspect becomes prominent in each gender. Parents treat children
of each sex differently from the moment of birth onward,
and the child internalizes these differences into its gender identity. Core gender identity, which is primarily
learned from the culture and augmented by biological factors, becomes permanently fixed around two-and-a-half
years of age, according to the research of Robert Stoller
(1968). Core gender identity shapes not only how one views

masculinity and femininity, but also one's body image, sense of self, and life goals.

During the Victorian era when Jung and Freud lived, those aspects of men which were considered unacceptable to their sense of masculinity were projected into women (Slipp 1993).

Men who were emotional or passive often were labeled as latent homosexuals, while women who were bright, active, and assertive were seen as penis envying, suffering a masculinity complex, or as femmes fatales who used their sexuality to emasculate men. We now can differentiate gender identity from sexual orientation. Gender identity is primarily learned from the cultural stereotypes that define what is masculine and feminine, and thus is in need of continuing external validation or reinforcement. On the other hand, sexual orientation is in most instances considered to be biologically inherited and permanently determines the choice of sexual object. An individual may have a solid gender identity as a male and still be attracted sexually to other men. Underlying Bly's appeal for men to retrieve the inner warrior is probably the fear of not being manly, of being a feminized momma's boy, which may be consciously or unconsciously equated with being homosexual.

## ISSUES OF NATURE VERSUS NURTURE

Boys are born with a greater amount of testosterone than women, which is responsible for the larger musculature in men and their higher level of aggression. From an early age, young boys engage in more rough-and-tumble play than girls. However, there are individual variations, and some men are gentler and some women are physically rougher. Some naturalists (Lorenz 1966) believe that male aggression in animals is adaptive in the struggle for survival. Male aggression in animals defines leadership dominance, establishes territories, provides food, protects the herd from predators, and allows the strongest males to reproduce. In reviewing the history of all cultures, Maccoby and Jacklin (1974) found that males commit a great many more acts of personal violence and organized social aggression than women. In a study of over four thousand Vietnam veterans, Dabbs and Morris (1990) noted that higher levels of testosterone were associated with delinquency, substance abuse, conflicts with authority, greater sexual activity, or dominance. However, the level of testosterone was found to fluctuate by as much as 30 percent in a study by Booth and colleagues (1989), falling after defeat and rising after victory in competitive sports.

Despite this biological potential for aggression in the male, the environmental context seems to play a more significant role. This adaptability to the environment has enabled humans to be more capable of survival than animals, which are basically driven by biological instincts. In many cultures, such as the Bushmen of South Africa, the Pygmies of the Ituri Forest, Eskimos, Australian aborigines, and others, there is no heritage of aggressive territoriality or war. Thus, even though there is a greater potential for aggressive and violent behavior in men, it is the cultural context that determines whether or not, and also the manner in which aggression is expressed. Similarly, therapy can also strongly influence and shape how individuals deal with frustration and conflict and manage aggressive feelings toward others. Feelings of aggression need not be acted out, but can be verbalized and worked through or sublimated.

## PROBLEMS IN GENDER THEORY

Therapists who need to deal with gender issues are faced with a psychological theory about gender relationships that is based on an antiquated nineteenth-century Victorian culture, which was phallocentric and patriarchal, steeped in a deep gender bias against women, and considered the development of women's personality as inferior to that of men. The main psychological theory of masculinity and femininity that existed up until recently was that developed by Sigmund Freud (1931), who himself was a product of a patriarchal and phallocentric culture. In addition, Freud's preoedipal relationship to his mother was very traumatic, and may have caused problems in separation from her and in his own gender identity formation (Slipp 1993). Probably because of these factors, Freud denied the role of the mother in his theory of early child development, considered both sexes as bisexual, and confused gender identity with sexual orientation.

Freud's difficulty separating from his mother continued into adulthood, but this was also influenced by the culture. Victorian women had little opportunity to achieve an identity of their own, and had to live vicariously through men's achievements. Since Freud's father was an economic failure, his mother needed to live through her son, and exploited Freud's achievement to feed her self-esteem. However, she was unable to be emotionally nurturant to him. Two causes for this lack of maternal nurturance may have been the need for women to have large numbers of children due to the high infant mortality rate, and the lack of contraceptives. Therefore most children received little individual attention. Another reason probably was the unconscious envy and hostility of women toward men, who diminished and imprisoned women in a stereotyped identity.

Freud's theory of personality development denied early attachment to the mother as a person and saw her only as an object to gratify the child's oral instincts. Freud focused on a boy's relationship with his father during the oedipal period (4 to 6 years of age) and its resolution due to the fear of castration. Freud believed the first internalization of a parent was the father, after the resolution of the Oedipus complex, which formed the superego or conscience. Female psychology was viewed from a male perspective, with penis envy as its cornerstone. Freud thought that since girls did not suffer castration anxiety like boys, women had difficulty resolving the Oedipus complex and thus had an inferior superego.

This classical psychoanalytic theory was first challenged by his colleague, Sandor Ferenczi, and then by neo-Freudian, Kleinian, object relations, and self psychology psychoanalysts. Freud's view of early child development has also not held up under the scientific scrutiny of direct infant observational studies. Rewriting psychoanalytic theory from a metapsychological–theoretical to an empirical–scientific perspective has occurred. The current focus is on the preoedipal mother–child relationship from birth to about 4 years of age. This is when separation from the mother takes place, boundaries between self and others are established, and gender identity develops.

For boys, separation from the mother is earlier than for girls, since boys need to establish a male gender identity. In addition, boys genetically seem to exhibit more rough-and-tumble behavior, making this period of separation more difficult for parents. Many parents are unaware that the oppositionalism of the child during the "terrible twos" is related to the need to separate and to establish ego boundaries. Instead, the child is often seen as bad and is punished. Since boys tend to be less verbal and more active than girls, they may suffer more physical punishment, and thus repress their feelings and act out more in their search for autonomy from a preoedipal mother who is seen as omnipotent and controlling. In turn, the mother may feel rejected by her son, and, feeling excluded, may herself turn away from him. The oedipal period has been emphasized in classical psychoanalysis, and now modern psychoanalysis focuses on the preoedipal period. However, the postoedipal period is also important, as mentioned by Erik Erikson (1963) and by studies in family therapy.

## FAMILY DYNAMICS—OBJECT RELATIONS MARITAL AND FAMILY THERAPY

My own work (Slipp 1984, 1988) has acknowledged the importance of these early preoedipal and oedipal periods, but has focused on the postoedipal relationships within the family and the society. The relationship with the parent is a continuing panphasic one that exerts influence on the child's identity formation, self-esteem, and ability to separate, achieve autonomy, yet remain connected.

If the parents prevent the child from establishing a life of his/her own or are neglectful or abandoning, these become vulnerable areas later in adult life. These issues are resurrected in a marriage when physical and emotional intimacy is established with one's spouse, as had previously occurred with the mother or father. Problems arise if one partner attempts to control and define the other in order to master childhood trauma. The result is a lack of regard for the other person's needs, and an invasion of boundaries. This is especially important for men, since women have an easier time during childhood development. Girls may suffer less punishment, since they are less involved in rough-and-tumble play and are more verbal than boys. Girls can also maintain their relationship with their mothers and separate gradually, since that relationship facilitates and does not threaten their gender identity.

Object relations theory is a way of integrating how childhood developmental traumas and arrests influence family functioning. My book, *Object Relations: A Dynamic Bridge Between Individual and Family Treatment* (1984), was the first book published in the United States on object relations family therapy. It introduced concepts from the British object relations and Kleinian schools of psychoanalysis for marital and family therapy in this country. It also described my research involved in developing a family typology that is related to psychopathology in the child.

My second book, *The Technique and Practice of Object Relations Therapy* (1988), dealt with treatment. It incorporated the techniques of psychoanalytic family therapy and those of systemic family treatment, such as feedback in the here and now and reframing. Unlike other forms of family therapy, my approach takes into account the family as a whole system, interpersonal relations, and intrapsychic dynamics. Object relations theory is used as the bridge between these various levels.

Through the primitive defenses of splitting and projective identification, internalized object relations of one or both parents are parceled out to family members, creating an unconscious collusive family system. Splitting involves seeing self or other as all good or all bad. In projective identification, a more primitive defense, unconscious interactional pressure, is exerted on the other person to enact the split-off good or bad aspects of the internal self or object representations. Here, the other person's ego boundaries are violated, and intrapsychic conflict gets displaced into the interpersonal sphere. The more mature defense of projection influences only how one perceives another person.

Both projective identification and repression get rid of unacceptable aspects. Projective identification is interpersonal, since one's ego boundaries are weak, and the other's boundaries are not respected. Repression is intrapsychic, since ego boundaries remain intact and unacceptable aspects are put into one's own unconscious. Through splitting and projective identification, a symbiotic survival pattern (Slipp 1969, 1973) is formed that violates individual boundaries, sustaining the self-esteem or personality integrity of the parents. Family group cohesion is thus preserved, but at the expense of individual autonomy.


## AN EXAMPLE
## OF PROJECTIVE IDENTIFICATION

A married man raised in a very strict and punitive manner continues to have difficulty asserting himself with his mother. Even though his mother does not have any power over him now and his survival is no longer at stake, he still feels programmed to relate to her as he did during childhood. When the mother visits, she criticizes the couple's way of childrearing, rearranges their furniture, and interferes with their decisions. Because the husband does not set limits on his mother's violation of the couple's boundaries, the wife is provoked into challenging the mother. When an argument ensues, the husband then blames his wife for not getting along with his mother and always putting him in the middle. He takes the safe middle ground so he can have his cake and eat it too. First, he provokes his wife into expressing his anger for him and lives vicariously through her. He does not need to take responsibility for expressing his own feelings and risk punishment or rejection by his mother. Second, he preserves his undifferentiated relationship with his mother. Third, he can displace his split-off anger onto his wife by inducing guilt and blaming her.

## COURSE OF TREATMENT

### Engagement

In either individual, couples, or family therapy, it is essential to establish rapport and trust, so that people can lower their defensiveness and honestly reveal their thoughts and feelings. A therapeutic contract and framework are established that set up boundaries for the conditions of treatment. This includes the time and place of treatment, the fee, and the procedures of treatment so that their goal can be achieved. The therapist does not take sides, does not assume a controlling, directive, or manipulative approach, but is impartially empathic. In this way *a safe holding environment* is established so that the patients can develop a *therapeutic alliance* and respect the therapist's perspective so as to seriously consider the interventions that are made.

## Past History

A history of the conflict is obtained along with ways they have attempted to deal with it. In addition, a history of the childhoods experienced in the parents' families of origin is taken, since it is helpful in noting the vulnerable areas and patterns of relationships that may be significant currently.

## Working with the Systemic Level

In couples and family therapy (Slipp 1988), the systemic level is dealt with first. The therapist can describe how their defensive interaction with each other establishes a *circular feedback cycle* that only escalates conflict. For example, when a husband is distant, the wife may feel rejected and become critical. In response, the husband becomes even more distant, and then the wife is even more critical. This pattern of interaction is clarified as, although defending one's position, only increases the conflict, so that no one wins. Each may become entrenched in his or her position and be unable to relate to the other and resolve the conflict.

## Working with Projective Identification

In the middle part of therapy, projective identification is interpreted, to establish boundaries in the couple's or family's interpersonal relationship. The interpretation of projective identification is made in an empathic and non-critical manner as follows:

1. The purpose of the projective identification is *reframed* into positive terms.
2. The *motivation* for its origin is empathically tied to childhood experiences.

For example, in the above example of a married couple, the therapist may state how the wife was *helpful* to her husband in setting limits with his mother, since he had difficulty asserting himself because he was raised strictly during childhood. He learned that any self-assertion or anger on his part was seen as bad and punished severely, and had to be repressed out of conscious awareness. Thus, his wife was providing him with help in this area until now. In this interpretation the husband is not scapegoated as a villain for using his wife, and the wife is reframed from scapegoat into savior. The husband understands why he needed to split off his aggression and to have his wife express these feelings for him so he could live vicariously through her. His unconscious feelings are brought to conscious awareness and he is given permission to take responsibility for his own feelings. He may even feel more masculine in not needing to be dependent on his wife to be assertive.

## Reowning Projective Identification and Working Through

The last phase, when family members reown their projective identification, is conducted on an intrapsychic level. Either in couples or individual therapy, there is an opportunity for each member to work through conflicts and developmental arrests. Working through needs to be done repeatedly in order to change brain circuitry and change behavior permanently.

## Termination

The members can then each mourn their losses and traumas and accept others' and their own limitations as they terminate treatment.

## Countertransference

During this process, therapists need to be aware of their own countertransference reactions. These reactions may be derived from the therapist's own unresolved issues or else be induced by the patient's projective identification. In either instance, the therapist is sucked into the system to collude with the unconscious external or internalized object relationships. For example, the husband in the above example of couples therapy may try to induce the therapist into viewing his wife as an aggressive and hostile person who cannot get along with his mother, and portray himself as a victim. If the therapist has had problems with women in his/her own life or goes along with old cultural biases against women showing anger, the therapist may form an alliance with the husband against the wife. Alternatively, even if the therapist is free from unresolved problems with women, the husband may try to influence the therapist's reaction to the wife subtly through projective identification. He may indicate that his wife is overreacting emotionally, suffers from PMS, and is hostile to his mother. The therapist thus needs to be sensitive to his or her emotional reaction to the wife, explore it, and not be induced to feel hostile to her. Only in this way will impartial empathy be maintained, boundaries established between the couple, and the husband have an opportunity, after projective identification is interpreted, to reown this split-off aspect of himself and then work it through.

## THE FAMILY TYPOLOGY

A typology of family relations was developed in my research at Bellevue Psychiatric Hospital in New York (see Figure 5–1). The typology is an example of the symbiotic survival pattern in the family, where individual boundaries are violated and autonomy sacrificed for the group. Four specific types of splitting and projective identification in the family dynamics were correlated with four specific types of psychopathology in the child. These were not considered causative, since they might arise out of inborn genetic defects. For example, in schizophrenia there may be a genetic fragility or lack of constancy of internalized object relations. This would explain why anger in schizophrenia might be experienced as destructive and

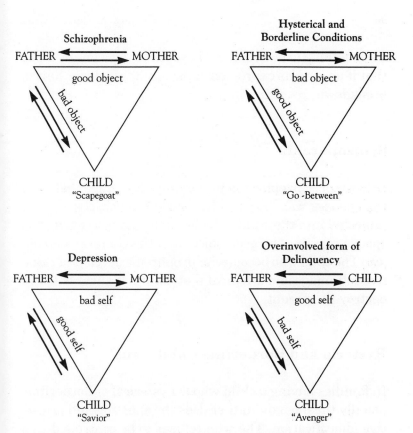

FIGURE 5–1. Categorization of family interaction. The father is indicated as the initiator of splitting and projective identification in all four patterns for purposes of simplicity. The mother may just as well be the initiator, except in hysterical and borderline conditions, in which the child is female. Projective identification is used as the intrapsychic and interpersonal defense mechanism that induces others to act out the internalized self or object image. The child serves as a container for the parent's projective identification, and a negative feedback cycle is thus established that (1) maintains the personality integrity of the parents, (2) maintains the family homeostasis, or balance of defenses, and (3) sustains developmental fixation in the patient. In all these instances the child is made responsible for the self-esteem and, in schizophrenia and borderline conditions, the survival of the parent(s), thereby establishing a symbiotic survival pattern. In one type of delinquency, splitting and projective identification of the bad self into one child and the good self into another child occurs. (From S. Slipp [1984], *Object Relations: A Dynamic Bridge between Individual and Family Treatment.* Jason Aronson. Used by permission.)

as something to be avoided. There was often a family myth that if anger was expressed, a parent would die or have a breakdown, resulting in loss.


## Schizophrenia

In cases of schizophrenia in a young adult, anger between the spouses was found to be split off unconsciously and projected into the child, who becomes the *scapegoat*. The spouse remains the good object and the child the bad object. The child who becomes schizophrenic develops a negative self-image and is fearful that his or her anger will also destroy the parent.


## Hysteria and Borderline Conditions

In families having a child who is hysterical or borderline, usually the husband/father does the splitting and projective identification. The wife refuses to be controlled as a need-satisfying good object for her husband. However, to maintain autonomy, the wife withdraws and is demeaned as the bad object by the husband, who turns to a child, usually the daughter, who satisfies the father's narcissistic needs and who is treated as the good object. This is experienced by the daughter as an oedipal triumph. The boundary between fantasy and reality is breached, leading to difficulty in impulse control. The daughter then functions as a *surrogate spouse* for the father, or *go-between*. Here the daughter also serves the function of sustaining the family integrity but at the expense of her individual autonomy. The daughter who becomes hysterical is not rejected and repeats what was done to her with others by sexualizing relationships to obtain dependency gratification. The child destined to become borderline is subsequently rejected, which leads to difficulty in impulse control, to sexualizing relationships, and to feeling worthless, discardable, and suicidal.

## Depression

In families with a depressive child, one spouse is seen as a failure and the child is pressured by the other spouse to compensate by succeeding socially. The failed spouse is perceived unconsciously as the bad self and the child as the good self. The child serves as a *savior,* through whom the dominant parent can live vicariously to sustain self-esteem. The dominant parent threatens rejection for failure but does not gratify the child's success. The dominant parent owns the success so that the child cannot grow confident but remains hungry and dependent because of lack of affirmation. I have called this a *double bind on achievement,* since the child cannot win whether he or she succeeds or fails.

## Overinvolved Delinquency

Although we did not research families with an overinvolved delinquent, that situation also fits the typology, as described by the work of Adelaide Johnson and Stanislaus Szurek (1954). A parent's negative feelings are split off unconsciously and projected into a child, who socially acts out the bad self of the parent and becomes an *avenger.*

Various combinations of these patterns may be projected into the same or different children, and roles may
be reassigned temporarily or permanently. For example,
we found that in narcissistic personality disorders the
child was alternately idealized as the go-between or savior and then demeaned as the scapegoat. The narcissistic
person does to others what was done to him, alternately
idealizing and demeaning others. All these patterns prevent individuation, interfere with establishing ego boundaries, and contribute to ego weakness. These patterns
were found not to be limited to these forms of severe pathology, but were used at times by normal families, especially when they regress under stress to a symbiotic survival pattern.

## INITIAL INTERVIEW AND DIAGNOSIS

During the initial interview with a male patient, the therapist needs to make both an individual diagnosis according to *DSM-IV* and a family diagnosis using the above
typology. This is accomplished by obtaining a history of
the current situation, previous life experiences, and especially a thumbnail sketch of his family of origin. This
information will also help in determining whether boundaries between self and others are too rigid and closed or
too open. For example, if boundaries are too open, the
patient might fear being engulfed and his identity over-
whelmed, making group therapy too threatening until this
changes later in treatment. Supplementing individual
therapy with group or marital therapy is often helpful in
enabling the male patient to retain autonomy and sepa-

rateness yet be connected to others and feel a sense of belonging.

The patient's internalized world of object relations can also be hypothetically constructed by the therapist. For example, the internalized object relations will be determined by whether the parents were perceived as harsh, cruel, and rejecting or intrusive and controlling. The patient's perception may not always fit the reality, but it determines the internal world of his object relations. This will alert the therapist to the type of transferences the patient will form. From the presenting complaint and history, the therapist can then determine the type of defenses employed, for example, repression, avoidance, projection, distancing, splitting, or projective identification. Self-esteem and conflicts over masculinity can be estimated, which are helpful in determining the course of therapy. Positive aspects of the patient are looked at, such as the ability to be intimate and loving as well as being trusting and objective enough to establish a therapeutic alliance fairly early in treatment.

## INDIVIDUAL THERAPY WITH MEN

What can the therapist do to help men deal with the issues that they now confront? First of all, it is important to become familiar with the literature on gender. Even though some of these factors are discussed here in previous chapters, greater depth of knowledge can be obtained by reading the following books: *In a Time of Fallen Heroes*, by William Betcher and William Pollack (1993); *Men Are from Mars, Women Are from Venus*, by John Gray

(1992); *Men in Therapy*, by Richard L. Meth and Robert S. Pasick (1990); and my own book on gender issues, *The Freudian Mystique* (Slipp 1993). It is of primary importance for the therapist to be knowledgeable and sensitive to gender issues.

In order to deal with your own countertransference, it is helpful to examine the gender socialization that existed in your own family of origin. Was your father the dominant one? What was your mother's role and in what areas was she empowered? How were girls raised differently than boys? What gender stereotypes were fostered? In treatment the therapist needs to encourage sharing, mutual responsibility, respect for boundaries, and sensitivity to each spouse's needs.

Challenging the traditional gender stereotypes is necessary, since they are no longer functional and contribute to conflict in modern families. For example, it is important for fathers to share in childrearing, to bond with their sons and daughters, and to be emotionally available and nurturing. This will prevent "father hunger" and hostility to men or its displacement onto authorities. Boys will not need to demean or control women, or to erect narcissistic defenses to deny emotions, dependency, and intimacy. For girls, good relationships with their fathers will reinforce confidence in their femininity, empower them to achieve, and enable them to trust men as genuine friends.

Men can learn that, like women, they are also constrained by traditional stereotypes and values. Many men need to be helped out of a repressed and isolated lifestyle, cut off from their feelings. They will not need women to express their repressed emotions for them, but can reown these emotions and become more complete human beings.

Hostility to the other sex will be reduced, bringing peace to the gender wars.

The same method of interpreting projective identification used in couples and marital therapy can be employed in individual therapy, that is, to *reframe* the purpose of the projective identification into a positive light that is not accusatory. The interpretation is connected to childhood experiences to understand the *motivation* that made it necessary for the man to repress certain feelings. This might be his need to split off feelings such as assertions or anger to avoid disapproval, punishment, or rejection. The need to split off and project certain emotions may not come only from the family but may also be culturally determined. For example, boys may be told that men don't cry, so unhappiness and grief are repressed.

By reframing the meaning of projective identification, the individual is not criticized for this limitation, since the therapist ties it in with an empathic understanding of where the need to split off and project unacceptable feelings comes from. The patient is not criticized and the other, usually the wife, is taken out of the scapegoat role and redefined into the role of savior. As mentioned above, the wife has been helping do what the patient was unable to do because of inhibiting circumstances in his childhood. When patients understand and accept the motivation for splitting off certain emotions, they may feel safe enough to own them and permit themselves to express them without the feared consequences. Additionally, the need not to be dependent for help on a woman to express split-off feelings may further mobilize the man to feel more masterful and autonomous. He can reown his split-off, unacceptable feelings and integrate them, instead of living vicariously through his wife and then condemning her.

## Illustrative Cases

In the following chapters, cases are selected to demonstrate certain family constellations from childhood that
produce later adult issues for men in relationships and
marriage. These include the legacies of a rejecting, powerful father; a controlling and seductive mother; the "gruesome twosome" parents who are overly involved with each
other and insensitive to their children's needs; an abandoning mother; an abandoning father; and conflicts in a
modern two-career family. A case of couples therapy is also
presented to illustrate the use of object relations therapy.

# 6

# Legacy of a Rejecting, Powerful Father

## THE CASE OF MR. RF

Mr. RF, a middle-aged businessman, came for individual therapy at the urging of his wife, since she was threatening to get a divorce unless he sought help. She had been in individual therapy herself for some time and could no longer tolerate being demeaned and feeling that she played second fiddle to her husband's business. She complained of poor communication and little intimacy or joy.

When I first saw Mr. RF, I could feel the tension he radiated. His jaw was clenched, and I felt he came into the office with his dukes up, ready for a fight. He was suspicious, hypervigilant, and clearly angry at being coerced to see a "shrink." I introduced myself and empathically tried to connect with him by acknowledging, "I can understand you really did not want to see me and came reluctantly because of your wife's insistence." He agreed that he was indeed resistant to coming. I said, "I can appreciate how you must feel, but since we are here together let's make the most of it and see if I can be of any help in our working out the marital difficulties between you and your wife."

He agreed, and said he felt alienated from his wife but did not want his marriage to end in divorce. He informed me of his previous two marriages and said that he had two children with each wife, and did not want to go through the trauma of another difficult divorce and be saddled with what would be six child support payments. He already was paying support to four children from these previous marriages. He felt attached to the two children from this marriage, and acknowledged that it would be difficult for him to start over again. He was older now and did not want to get into the singles scene again. He said, "It's not what I had imagined after my first divorce. I lost many of my married friends, and it's lonely out there. I hated all the time it took away from my work, and there were many disappointments."

We established a therapeutic contract concerning the time, payment of fees, and makeup for missed sessions, and I encouraged him to be as open and honest as possible in order to try to reach our agreed-upon goal of improving his marital relationship and avoiding a divorce. I asked him to tell me whatever came to mind, not to censor his thoughts, and if he had any dreams to bring them in, since they might reveal underlying issues that he was trying to resolve.

I then told him that I wanted to get as rounded a picture of him as a person as I could, and would like to start by getting some background information. I asked him for a thumbnail sketch of his parents and siblings when he was growing up, and his relationships with them. He told me his father was engrossed in his business, coming home tired in the evening and wanting to rest and be alone. He was a stern and silent man, not emotionally available, and at times explosively angry. His father was the dominant parent, making all the major decisions, as well as being the disciplinarian who did the punishing. Everyone, including his mother, tiptoed around his father.

The patient informed me he was born with some minor physical defects, which made his father feel ashamed of him. The father distanced himself from the patient, and preferred the older brother. Father would take his brother out fishing and played ball with him, but excluded the patient. Mr. RF was not athletic as a child, and the father made no effort to comfort or help him, but disdainfully nicknamed the patient "Chicken." The patient, without openly admitting it, intimated he felt demeaned, emotionally injured, and rejected by his father.

It became clear to me that the patient was never affirmed by his father and had developed a poor self-image, especially as a man. His mother was a traditional housewife, who was the social secretary and supervised the household. She was a compliant, detached, and self-preoccupied woman, who satisfied the patient's physical but not emotional needs.

The patient seemed to be what I have called an *emotional orphan* (Slipp 1988), having been deprived of mirroring during his childhood, and demonstrated a narcissistic personality disorder. He defended against poor self-esteem and a poor sense of masculinity, was walled off from intimate relationships, was distrustful of others, and had erected rigid ego boundaries. Although he seemed grandiose and powerful, his fragile self-esteem was vulnerable and dependent on constant external validation. If his feeling of narcissistic entitlement was not gratified or he felt rejected, his underlying anger emerged in a verbal assault.

When the father died, the brother took over the father's business and tried to eliminate the patient from any position of power. The brother had always felt special and superior to the patient, demeaning him as the father had done. The patient at the time was married and had two small children, and decided to fight for his share of the business. Mr. RF harnessed his underlying anger to summon up the strength to compete with his brother. The patient maneuvered himself to become indispensable to the business by developing personal relations with the major accounts. Eventually Mr. RF gained control of the business and excluded his brother.

The patient could not tolerate feeling helpless and unmanly, could not depend on others, and needed always to be in control. He always fought against anything that made him feel that he was "chicken," and developed a loner, self-sufficient, macho, and grandiose lifestyle. In his current marriage, he also had to be in control, treating his wife as if she were an employee or a sexual object to serve him. He did not share decision-making with her and gave her a weekly allowance to manage the house. If she did not do what he wanted or feed his vanity and sense of manliness, he would have bursts of anger and say hurtful things to her. She felt used, abused, and demeaned. (I kept in the back of my mind that his wife was being judged and abused just as he had been at the hands of his father.)

His wife distanced herself, stopped talking openly with him, and their sexual life ground to a halt. They had been married for ten years and had two small children. Mr. RF was a workaholic, married to his business, which had become very successful due to his dedicated efforts to prove himself a man. He was aware that there was a repetitious pattern, with his two previous wives getting angry at him for being what they called a "control freak." Interpersonal conflicts were not discussed, negotiated, or resolved with any of his wives. Each of his previous marriages ended in warfare and a bitter divorce. Mr. RF had little contact with his previous ex-wives or children, who were angry and alienated from him. However, he felt that he was the victim, and that they were selfish and demanding.

He came into sessions complaining about his current wife excluding him, and that his children seemed to side with her. He had some insight into the fact that he had a temper, but he seemed unaware of the demeaning impact it had on her. He could not empathize with her perspective. I listened without comment as he expressed his viewpoint.

A number of sessions later after a firm therapeutic alliance and a safe holding environment were established, I felt he would listen to an interpretation without feeling criticized and rejected. I reminded him of how sensitive he had felt when demeaned by his father, and how angry he felt over not being considered manly enough and at being judged critically by his father. (Mr. RF had projected the unacceptable weak, victimized part of himself into his wife, while identifying with the internalized aggressive and judgmental father in order to repeat and master the trauma.) I interpreted that since his father was his model for relationships, he unconsciously did to his wife what his father had done to him. He did this even though consciously he did not want to be like his critical and nonsupportive father. He recognized that he was enacting the same pattern as his father, but still felt his wife was really selfish and deserved to be put down.

On discussion in the next session, it became apparent that his wife was fearful of confronting him because of his temper, and had distanced herself and become self-protective. These issues were discussed, connecting how her behavior followed in the wake of his. Probably his father also felt justified in being unsympathetic to him as a child, and Mr. RF, like his wife, also felt diminished and angry. Perhaps he could understand that his wife was expressing the same kind of anger he also must have felt toward his father but was unable to deal with openly for fear of further rejection by his father. The goal was to repeatedly work this conflict through so as to enable Mr. RF to empathize and understand his wife's perspective and not to scapegoat her. He provoked her through projective identification into expressing for him the split-off anger he must have felt towards his father. I commented that his father had not been sensitive to Mr. RF's perspective and needs, but had been judgmental, condemning, and rejecting. This had been hurtful, and I was sure he consciously didn't want to repeat this same pattern with his wife.

In one of the later sessions he reported having had several anxiety dreams. "I'm walking alone at night, I'm afraid its getting late and I don't have a place to sleep. I can't find a taxi and feel completely lost." In the other dream, "I was traveling on a train and had a lot of luggage. I didn't have enough time to get all the luggage off the train. I get some of it off, but the train leaves with part of my luggage, and I go bananas." He openly admitted how as a child he felt unprotected by his father, could not depend on him, was frightened of him, and felt lost and alone. There was no one to help. His mother was preoccupied with household chores, insensitive to his needs, and he could not confide in her. His brother was domineering and competitive with him. He felt alone and had no support from anyone. He openly expressed his anxiety, fear, and frustrated dependency in this dream. The other dream suggested he was fearful that he had too much emotional baggage and wondered if he could depend on me to help him. He knew my summer vacation was coming up soon, and was fearful that his relationship with his wife had not improved sufficiently and that she would take the children and leave him.

Mr. RF became more aware of his dependency needs and was struggling with his ability to trust me as a good, nonabandoning father. He developed a warm relationship with me, and manifested a strong positive transference. Since he had been a loner all his life with his family and his peers, I suggested group therapy. I told him this would give him an opportunity to feel part of a family and community, since, as he told me, he had always felt like an outsider. My goals were to engage him in a socializing group experience, to teach him to be cooperative instead of being always competitive, to further sensitize him to other perspectives, and to give him feedback on his behavior.

With some reluctance he accepted, and joined my group. Although at first he tended to try to monopolize the group and be combative, competitive, and controlling, other group members confronted him and he monitored himself. He became aware of the effect he had on others through their constructive feedback, which sensitized him to cause and effect. This was also a learning experience on how to give feedback that was not personally demeaning but dealt with objective behavior.

As the members accepted him in subsequent sessions and he grew to become part of the group, he also developed an outside group of male friends, something he had never done. Previously he immersed himself in work and continued to isolate himself as he had in his family of origin. The outside male group also liked and accepted him for himself, and he became involved with them in playing racketball and having dinner afterward. He surprised himself by becoming a good athlete and was admired by this group of men. He was able to sublimate his competitive behavior and learned to share intimacy with his men's group. In these ways his "father and peer hunger" was gradually satisfied, and he learned to be cooperative instead of always distrustful and competitive. With further therapy, he became more sensitive to his wife's needs and was more willing to accept her limitations instead of always taking her behavior as a personal attack. He had seen her simply as angry and passive-aggressively trying to frustrate him.

He had been angry at her for not being his social secretary, just as his mother had been for his father. He had fought with his wife to get her to make social engagements, and had not taken on this role himself. I suggested that perhaps he feared that it might be perceived by others that he was not manly, that is, a "chicken," if he performed a role he believed that women should perform. I then discussed the changing role structure of the modern family, where these roles are now shared and not simply assigned by gender. Nowadays he would not be seen as unmanly if he ran the social calendar.

As therapy progressed, even though he was gentler and kinder and he took over the social calendar, Mr. RF still resented the time it took, since he was such a busy person. He commented, "Why didn't my wife take over this social responsibility? Previously I didn't take over the social calendar because that is what a wife is supposed to do. Why did my wife not want to accommodate to me?" He continued to take this personally and was judgmental and critical. He was now, however, able to bring this up to her, and she explained that she was very shy and unable to do it. He recognized that this might be the case. If he was critical and attacked her personally, it was like "beating a dead horse" and he needed to accept her human limitations.

When he demeaned his wife, it only angered her and alienated him from his children, who rallied to her defense. He did not get what he wanted, and he was alienated from his wife and children. As he became aware of the interaction, he acknowledged to her that he might be responsible for her lack of cooperation by the way he acted. She then told him that he embarrassed her socially by what he said to others. She said, "You make me seem like a pathetic waif to inflate your ego so you can appear like the big man." She had punished him by passive-aggressively provoking him to do something he did not consider masculine, be the social secretary. The punishment fit the crime. He promised to change, becoming more involved with his children from this marriage and those from his previous marriages.

In later sessions he talked about problems at work, especially of relationships with his employees. Some of his employees had been frightened of being "butchered and drawn and quartered" by him, and they had not communicated important problems about some of their accounts. When some of these accounts were lost, it became apparent that his anger had so intimidated his employees that they could not communicate with him. He then changed the way he gave feedback so that it was constructive and not personally demeaning. He made efforts to contain his anger, recognizing that it was self-defeating at work just as it had been at home. He was able to improve his com-

munication ability and deal with problems as they came
up, resulting in better functioning of his business as well.
Thus, this patient improved at home and in his business
relationships. His marriage survived, he had a supportive peer group of men, and he developed better relationships with all his children.

## TIPS ON WHAT TO DO AND WHAT TO AVOID

1. Make an empathic connection in the first and early
   sessions to facilitate engagement in therapy.
2. Work through resistance to treatment, especially
   when the patient was coerced into treatment, so as
   to lower defensiveness.
3. Establish a therapeutic contract about the terms of
   treatment and set goals to avoid later problems.
4. Interpretations need to be made at the right time,
   after a safe holding environment and a therapeutic
   alliance are established, to avoid their being taken
   as criticism, resisted, and rejected.
5. Avoid focusing solely on the here and now, which pre-
   vents the therapist from interpreting the old baggage
   the patient carries.
6. Help the patient be aware of his underlying poor self-
   esteem and masculine identity and his need to obtain the feedback from others he did not receive as a
   child.
7. Reown and consistently work through the projections
   of his inadequacies onto his wife, doing to her what
   his father did to him as a child.
8. Help the patient be sensitive to his effect on others,
   and to the self-defeating interaction that results.

# 7

# Legacy of a Controlling, Seductive Mother (Abusive Love)

## THE CASE OF MR. CM

Mr. CM was a 35-year-old lawyer who came for therapy on the advice of his girlfriend, who felt he had a fear of commitment. He and his girlfriend had been going steady for over a year, and their relationship had not progressed. Previously, he had had many affairs with women, but as soon as the question of love and marriage arose, he would find something wrong with the woman and distance himself. He had little awareness of his repressed feelings, and tended to rationalize and act out his conflict. Even his perception of the woman would change: she would no longer seem physically attractive to him. This would justify his breaking off relations with her and starting up with another woman.

Mr. CM told me he was aware of a repetitious pattern of fear of commitment (as his girlfriend had noted), and we agreed to work on that together. He felt he was getting older, and stated he wanted to get married and have a family. Our goal was to work on his phobia to enable him to make a commitment. When I obtained a family history later, it confirmed my initial impression that Mr. CM's ego boundaries seemed vulnerable to invasion, and he needed to distance himself for fear of engulfment. To provide a relationship with secure boundaries, a therapeutic framework was established concerning times, fee, and make-up appointments. Since he was not coerced into coming and seemed undefensive and apparently motivated to change, the engagement process would be shorter than for Mr. RF. I proceeded to obtain a family history, which he gave freely.

Mr. CM had a middle-class upbringing, with his father owning his own retail business. The business had been bought for him by his wife, who had inherited money from her family. She also was the bookkeeper and general manager of the business. Father had grown up in a small town in New Jersey, where the Nazi Bund had been strong prior to World War II. He was taunted and occasionally beaten up by bands of German youngsters because he was Jewish. Father also had a severe learning disability, which interfered with his ability to succeed academically or athletically, and he remained an outsider in school. Because of these childhood traumas, his father had low self-esteem and had a depressed and passive attitude towards life. Father was quite dependent on his wife because of his learning disability, which interfered with his memory and organizational ability.

The patient's mother was a bright and assertive woman, well organized, with an excellent memory, who could compensate for her husband's deficiencies. She had also had a traumatic childhood, her mother dying when she was a young girl and her father, who was a womanizer, giving her up for adoption. (I wondered to myself if there had been a seductive relationship before being rejected by her father.) In the new home the adoptive father was a strict, witholding, controlling, and punitive individual feared and detested by my patient's mother. She feared and did not trust men. She married her husband because he was a gentle soul, nonthreatening, who needed her. On the other hand, she resented his vulnerability and passivity, and expressed her stored-up anger at her rejecting father and adoptive father by demeaning him ruthlessly for not being more effective and protective. Mr. CM informed me that all his life he blamed his mother for his father's lack of vitality and initiative. "My father seemed like a dead man."

Mr. CM informed me that his mother was unhappy with her weak and unprotective husband, so she turned to her son, who became almost a surrogate husband. The patient's family dynamics fit in with the hysterical/borderline constellation, in which one parent turns seductively to a child for narcissistic supplies that are not obtained from the spouse. The patient was seductively bound to his mother and had hysterical and phobic features in his personality. His mother was overly attentive to him, coming into his room without knocking, tucking him in, puffing up his pillow, opening the window, and giving him a goodnight kiss and hug every night. This continued through his adolescence, despite the patient's strong vocal objections.

In the first few sessions, Mr. CM would enter my office without waiting to be invited in. I experienced this as an intrusion, since I was still writing my notes on the previous patient and was not ready for him. I recognized my frustration, contained it, and firmly but gently set limits on this by asking him to please wait in the waiting room

until I was ready for him. I then used my countertransference reaction to interpret his projective identification
of an aspect of himself into me. This was first reframed
in a positive light. I stated that when he came into my
office unannounced I could empathically understand how
he must have felt when his mother came into his bedroom
without knocking. This enabled him to own his anger and
not to provoke me to express it. In this situation, I recognized that my countertransference resulted from the patient doing to me what his mother had done to him. Thus,
boundaries were established, and the patient was able to
own his feelings and work them through instead of using
splitting and projective identification.

He recognized that his mother needed to keep him a
cuddly baby, and used her seductiveness to control him.
It was hard for him to grow up and to feel masterful, since
his mother was insensitive to his developmental needs.
In addition, he did not see his father as an adequate, manly
figure. The patient also protected his father when Mother
was too abusive and demeaning to him. He fought his
mother when she humiliated his father in an attempt to
maintain an idealized male image with whom he could
identify.

He expressed fear that he would become a dead man
like his father if he married, yet he was attracted to very
bright, efficient career women, who would plan ahead and
make decisions for him. He felt very comfortable; they
were like an old shoe, like his highly organized mother.
He felt loved and protected as he did with his mother, but
doubted his ability to make decisions. However, after a
short while these women would look unattractive to him.
He would distance himself, provoking the woman to break

off the relationship, and he would find another woman to repeat this cycle over and over again.

He was aware that all the women he went with complained that after a while a wall developed between them and his passion waned. He said, "I feel claustrophic when I get too close. I feel confined, like I will die. I recall being warned as a small child not to crawl into a refrigerator, where I would be asphyxiated." He associated the refrigerator with the fact that his mother was nurturant but too engulfing. He felt suffocated by her, as if he would lose his masculine identity and die as a person like his father. Therefore, he erected defensive barriers against women. His mother had not only been infantilizing, but had been seductive towards him, hugging and kissing him repeatedly. He informed me, "Up until I was 12 years old, she still wanted me to sit on her lap." She did not respect his objections, but only responded to her own needs. He felt his mother did not want him to grow up to be a strong, assertive man, whom she would fear like her adoptive father, but wanted him to remain a child. To feel safe, she needed to remain the dominant figure who pulled the strings and was in control. He felt he had engaged in splitting, defining men as either weak and gentle or strong and cruel. She also instilled distrust of women in her son and a sense of his inadequacy, fearing he would be taken advantage of by women.

In following sessions, the patient informed me that his mother turned her sensuality and need for affection towards him because she did not receive it from her husband. Mr. CM felt enraged because his wishes were not respected when he asked her to stop. She was seductive, and he had won an oedipal victory, but he did not admit enjoying it. The victory was conflictual, since it further diminished his father. Mr. CM said, "I had to establish the controls. She couldn't and my father was not protective." I commented that possibly part of him enjoyed the oedipal victory, since nearly all boys have these oedipal wishes towards their mothers. However, another part of him probably felt threatened by the oedipal victory, since his mother blurred the boundary between playful fantasy and reality. Mother's affection was in response to her needs and not the patient's, and it also interfered with his being able to identify with his father. He said, "Some children are physically abused, but I was abused by love."

The patient related that there were many likeable things about his father, even though he seemed a joyless, depressed human being. He was never abusive and was respectful and considerate. Father was not mechanically inclined, because of his learning disability, but he was sweet, considerate, and gentle. For example, his father helped Mr. CM establish a relationship with a neighboring man, who had a machine shop in his garage. Father also bought the patient a bike that he wanted, and would attend sporting events in which Mr. CM participated.

The patient stated, "When Father was away from my mother he seemed to function more adequately, so I blamed my mother for all his weaknesses, but now I realize that he probably was depressed and passive even before he married my mother. He had such a difficult childhood because of anti-Semitism, his learning disability, and because his mother also was the dominant one and his father was also passive. His father was an immigrant and could not earn enough, so his wife had to take in sewing and take over responsibility."

Mr. CM then talked about his relationship with his girl-friend. He said, "She can reach down into my soul. We communicate deeply, and she can be my best friend, yet she complains of a lack of love on my part." He explored his feelings and revealed that he had sadistic feelings towards women. Once the woman cares, he can withold and exert power over them. "It's a form of revenge against my powerful mother and women in general." I commented, "I guess you can turn the tables. You can render them powerless, like you felt with your mother when you were growing up." (This is an example of projective identifica-tion of his weak self onto the women and then punishing them by witholding what they needed.) He said, "Even with my mother the best way of punishing her was to dis-tance myself. It turned the tables. She was the one who felt frustrated and helpless, not me." He said, "My girl-friend is in many ways like my mother, controlling and invasive, and I need to push her away to breathe."

At this point in therapy, he distanced himself further from his girlfriend. She became angry and felt that unless he presented her with an engagement ring, they should not see each other any more. She was tired of the ups and downs in their relationship. He said, "She didn't want to see me any more unless I made a commitment. I realize I have a lot of anger at women and like to torture and hurt them. Even my work as a lawyer means working on the edge of cruelty, defeating the opposition or eviscerating and impeaching a witness." I suggested that perhaps his pulling away from his girlfriend was not only to hurt her but to also protect her from his sadistic feelings.

As he became more aware of acting out his unconscious sadistic feelings towards his mother and women in general, his resistance to inner exploration diminished. He then was able to talk about and gradually work through these feelings. He recalled how angry he had been at his mother, even having fantasies of killing her. He went so far as to consider ways of doing away with her. He said, "I remember never being left alone, my privacy was invaded constantly, and she tortured me with her need for affection. It was too much. She also didn't like my friends and insulted them when they came to the house. I felt humiliated and my friends and I called her the Wicked Witch of the West. I ran away from home several times, one time overnight. I wanted to be manly, not a wimp. I even got into fights at school, and I think I wanted to be bad to rub her nose in it. She couldn't control me—I showed her by my actions. My father let her have all the power. He abdicated his role as a man.

"I recall having a fantasy of having a remote control that would shut her up. Instead of feeling violent towards her, I withdrew. It was the only way of hurting her, by withdrawing. She was unstoppable. I fear dominating women who try to control every aspect of my life. I fight to maintain some autonomy. I felt she was trying to make me into a wimp like my dad. A man who she would not be afraid of, who is compliant, and not aggressive. My mother couldn't tolerate masculine men, yet she hated weak men. Her father who gave her up for adoption was weak, and her adoptive father was aggressive and abusive. She needed to weaken a man, but then she didn't respect him."

He noted that his mother was also rejecting of all his high-school and college girlfriends. There was always something wrong with them. "She feared that women would take advantage of me and couldn't be trusted." He said, "She was always hugging and kissing me, and I felt

I needed to break away, to run away. I felt trapped and claustrophobic with her. It was as if I wasn't entitled to a life of my own, but I needed to make my mother happy. Even though at times I enjoyed her attention, it was too much, and stifling. I never felt like a separate person from my mother; she was only sensitive to what she needed. I only felt like an entity that she needed to control and to feed her needs. Even though I got so much attention from my mother, I wound up feeling empty, since it was not what I needed. I couldn't fill the void that my mother felt from her childhood, and I hope that I don't repeat it with my children and use them to fill my void."

In the next session, he said, "I'm really afraid that I might repeat this same behavior with my kids, give them too much love because I need it myself, but I know I'd try to be sensitive to their needs and constrain myself. I have to recognize and respect the boundaries between them and myself. I'm concerned that my girlfriend may use sex as a way of trying to control me, just as my mother did with her seductive behavior. If I don't accede to my girlfriend's sexual needs she gets angry. I think she also was probably not nurtured as a child by her parents, like my mother, and uses sex to gain affection and attention. I feel I have to comply to make her happy. Then when I feel controlled by my girlfriend, I resent it, since sex becomes a power issue and is not spontaneous and enjoyable.

"When I was growing up my father exerted no control at all, and even though my mother was controlling, at least somebody was at the helm. If she didn't control we'd be helplessly adrift. So I have ambivalent feelings about my mother's exerting control. My father also felt helpless and needed her to be in control. He couldn't remember telephone numbers, couldn't organize and manage his business, and was very unmechanical. I resented his being weak like that, but viewed myself as also being similar to him. Like my father, we needed her to keep life organized and to protect us from the world, or we would be lost. But I also hated her being on top of me, and for adding to my feeling emasculated."

He said, "There's a primordial part of me that feels safe with a woman like my mother, but I don't feel competent. When my girlfriend and I are with friends, she monopolizes the conversation and steals the limelight, which I resent." I restated and clarified his conflict, that with his mother he felt safe, yet it was at the expense of his feeling like a competent man. He agreed and felt his mother emasculated him even though she provided the only security in the family.

In the next session he reported having read the book *The Road Less Traveled* and felt his world view is associated with not feeling capable of meeting life's challenges, which results in his feeling miserable. He had doubts about his being able to be a man, handle responsibilities of a family, and have control over his life. He was fearful that he was like his father or would become like him if he married, and be a dead man, depressed and hopeless.

He then had the insight that it was his father's choice to seek security at the price of his masculinity and self-respect. He had no confidence in himself. But he said, "I am different, I know, I don't need a woman to help me survive like my father. He was doomed right from his childhood. I have insight and choice. I know I'm at the crossroads. I wish you could tell me what to do. I know my girlfriend is not perfect. Tell me: Should I commit to her or not?" I replied that if I made the decision for him, I'd be like his mother, taking over and controlling, and he would resent it. I knew it was difficult, but it was a life decision and only he could make it.

In the next session, he reported a dream. "I was being examined by a surgeon for nothing that was serious or life-threatening. His nurse was going to do a lung biopsy. She took cotton and stuffed up my nose and ears, and then pulled my nose. The nurse knew I didn't need to go through this. I then told them that I really didn't need this procedure. I needed to assert myself, which I did, and the surgeon, who was not evil, did not do the procedure." He associated the dream to his relationship with his girlfriend, feeling guilty that he could not make up his mind about committing to her. The lung biopsy had to do with being able to breathe and speak, with not being suffocated. The cotton up his nose made him fearful he would be intubated and put to sleep for no good reason. The nurse reminded him of himself, his observing self. The surgeon reminded him of his girlfriend, who is domineering and aggressive, a "clone" of his mother. He said, "I feel I'll be suffocated, raped, and my masculinity will be injured. Although I feel secure and safe with a domineering woman, it's as if there is a role reversal, and I feel inadequate and my manliness is injured. I asserted myself and felt better in the dream."

He informed me, "I told my girlfriend, who's also in therapy, about my dominant mother and weak father, a mother who provided security but emasculated my father. I had the same fear. My mother also humiliated my father in front of me, tried to infantilize me and keep me from growing into a strong man, and that I was dealing with my anger at my mother and women in general. That night my girlfriend had a nightmare. She said in the dream I was a cruel, wild-eyed person who told her I was

gay and locked her in a closet. She called for her mother
to come and rescue her. I let her out of the closet and raped
her on a hard cement floor. She hit her head in the dream
and awoke crying. She said she was reacting to my statement that I like masculine women who emasculate men,
that I feel safe with them. She thought that she also had
problems with men, like my mother, fearing their anger
and preferring to go with passive men. Our pathologies
meshed, she said, although she is trying to change herself in therapy to trust men."

The fact that his girlfriend admitted responsibility for
her own problems in their relationship tended to equal-
ize things between them. It was now a level playing field.
She made more efforts to work out her fear of men in her
own therapy, and did not put all the blame on him. The
patient then expressed his fear that if he were an adequate
and strong male, his mother and his girlfriend might not
continue to love him. He felt that was a condition of their
relationship, that kept them connected, and he feared
abandonment if he were strong and autonomous.

In subsequent sessions the patient continued to work
through his problems with his domineering and seductive
mother and unprotective father and how they affected his
fear of commitment. He saw marriage as his being enslaved and drained, with nothing in it for him. He said,
"I'd become a pack animal loaded down with the responsibilities of a family on my back." I interpreted that possibly he had developed the expectation of giving and not
getting for himself because he felt his mother satisfied her
needs but was not sensitive to his. He had wanted affection but on his terms, not constantly as dictated by his
mother's needs. He agreed and felt his father also did not
get his needs met, being just a slave to her as well and to

family responsibility. However, he was also aware that his father never asserted his needs.

The patient believed the only way to express his anger and not be exploited was to withdraw or break off the relationship. He did not want his mother to abandon him totally, but he did not always want to feel compelled to give in to what she demanded. (He had seen his relationship with her in black-and-white terms, that is, used splitting.) He had the same expectations of marriage, that his needs would not be met at all. He would end up with an empty pit in his stomach, while taking on the responsibility of satisfying his wife's and children's needs. He then recognized he was not a small, dependent child fearful of abandonment or engulfment, he was a free adult. He was entitled to stand up for his own needs, just as his wife could stand up for hers. But he did not have to give in or withdraw, he could negotiate, and each could accommodate to the other. Marriage could be nurturing and joyful for him as well.

He recognized that his mother had given him a double-level message, to be strong and manly on a conscious verbal level but interfering with his growing up and needing to keep him a dependent child on a behavioral level. His mother had transmitted her ambivalence about weak and dominant men to the patient, invading his boundaries. She projected her own fear that other women, like herself, would dominate and emasculate him. She also did not want him to grow up and be strong and independent and then leave her. He was to remain a boy, like Peter Pan, deprived of an adult life of his own. He recognized that he needed to comply with his mother, to be indecisive and weak. If he were confident and competent, which he really was as an adult man, he feared loss of love and abandonment by his mother. But by giving in to her demands, he felt engulfed and lost his autonomy and sense of masculinity. This internalized relationship with his mother determined his current relationships with women. By entering into temporary relationships with women, he got his emotional and sexual needs met, but could distance himself and escape being engulfed and enslaved.

In the following session he reported a dream, which became a turning point. "My girlfriend and I are in an old house from Revolutionary days. I dread something bad will happen. Some witches appear and take my girlfriend away, and I bargain with them to get her back. I pretend they have me in their power. They bring my girlfriend back, and I put my foot on her neck to hold her down. A witch gives me a razor blade to cut her, and instead I slice the face of the witch and peel her face off. A white ooze comes out."

He associated to the dream. "I was worried that I would hurt my girlfriend with my foot on her neck, but it was necessary to win the confidence of the witch. My mother is the witch and doesn't want me to leave and have a relationship with a woman. The other witches are my own internal demons from whom I want to revolt. My mother presented all women as villains, and said that I would become a victim like my father, taken over and controlled. But it's my mother who is like Darth Vader, taken over by the forces of evil, encased in a shell, cut off from adult loving relationships, unstoppable, and powerful. In one of the *Star Wars* movies, Luke Skywalker unmasks him, like I did with the witch, and discovers a distorted shrunken human underneath. The white ooze is as if she were a bloodless, mechanical monster, and I also want to get rid of the demon that is inside me. I suspect my mother's father was a ladykiller, and my mother also wants me to be a ladykiller like him. I can have affairs, but she's always been critical of every woman I have gone with. But I'm not supposed to leave and abandon my mother like her father did."

The patient then decided to make a commitment to his girlfriend and bought her an engagement ring. There continued to be ups and downs in therapy, as he worked through his insights. During this time he also became more empathic and understanding of his parents, integrating his ambivalence toward them as well. He recognized that it was not the marriage itself or his mother who was to blame, but that his father had always been a joyless and depressed individual even during his childhood. Both his parents had strengths and weaknesses, and both had been wounded and crippled by their childhoods. Even though he would not want a marriage like theirs, it worked for them, since his parents' personality problems fit together and were complementary.

Mr. CM recognized he had come from a family that did not recognize individual boundaries. His parents had suffered deficits in their childhood development and needed to use others to fill their emptiness. Mr. CM also felt empty and sought a strong woman in order to feel whole. Both his parents and the patient used and did not respect the needs of others as separate persons. Not only were the boundaries of others invaded, but Mr. CM also feared that he too would be invaded and his sense of self lost. He no longer wanted to do to others what had been done to him. Boundaries of others and his own needed to be respected, which allowed Mr. CM to enter an intimate relationship.

## TIPS ON WHAT TO DO AND WHAT TO AVOID

1. Avoid taking a directive role, even though the patient seems to want to induce this countertransference response from the therapist. Being directive would not differentiate the therapist from the mother, making interpretation of this transference difficult. It would reinforce dependency and the need for a dominant mother, which he would then resent and defensively withdraw from. This would recreate a vicious cycle of acting out, just as with the women in his life. It would not support his autonomy and masculinity, and would perpetuate his not being assertive and responsible.

2. Maintain an empathic but neutral stance and avoid siding with the patient against his controlling mother. Siding against his mother would only reinforce his splitting and seeing her only as the all-bad parent, responsible for the emasculation of the father. The patient needs to express his feelings, integrate his ambivalence, individuate, and accept her limitations as a person.

3. Avoid siding with the patient against his weak father, who did not protect him from an intrusive mother. Siding would perpetuate splitting, prevent integration of ambivalence, and not differentiate him from his father.

4. Avoid siding with the patient against his girlfriend, who had problems trusting men and chose a man needing a domineering woman. Their psychological needs for distance meshed with each other, but also provoked conflict and sustained pathology.

5. Avoid simply focusing on the here-and-now relationship with his girlfriend, since baggage from his childhood (being controlled and exploited for his mother's needs) interfered with his ability to be intimate and make a commitment, and led him to act out his anger by withdrawing.

6. Avoid going along with the patient's fantasy that he only needed to find the right girlfriend, which he used to avoid focusing on unconscious conflicts about needing but also fearing a dominant woman. Becoming aware that the problem is within him would enable the patient not to act out the conflict with his mother with other women. Recognizing and verbalizing his feelings enables him to work through his ambivalence about a loving but intrusive mother and his fears of engulfment or abandonment by her.

# 8

# Legacy of Abandoning Parents: The Gruesome Twosome

## THE CASE OF MR. AP

Mr. AP was an accountant in his late thirties, whose wife urged him to get into therapy since she was unhappy in their marriage. They had two children and had been married for about ten years. The joy and excitement had left their marriage, and they had become distant and uncommunicative. He seemed motivated to come, since he recognized he was cut off from his feelings and knew deep down that he could have a better marital relationship. He was able to be emotionally available and responsive to his children but not to his wife. He readily made a therapeutic contract concerning hours, missed appointments, and fee. Our goal was to help him get in touch with himself and to relate better to his wife. Diagnostically he seemed also to be an "emotional orphan" (Slipp 1988) and to have features of a narcissistic personality disorder. His ego boundaries seemed semipermeable, blocking out his wife and other adults but admitting his children, to whom he was connected. After the first few months of treatment, the patient was engaged and a therapeutic alliance had been established.

He described his family of origin as being "a house of strangers." His father had grown up in poverty during the Depression, and apparently was traumatized by overseas combat while in the Army during World War II. His main goal was to provide economic security for the family, but aside from that concern he was detached emotionally from his children. Mr. AP's mother had lost her brother in the Army in World War II, and shortly thereafter her father died. She never confronted and mourned their losses and had difficulty investing emotionally in others. The patient stated she was like the mother in the movie *Ordinary People,* who could not get over the accidental death of one son and rejected the living son. She was not emotionally available or protective of her children, but she was devoted to her husband's needs. She also had a semipermeable ego boundary, but the opposite of the one the patient developed in his marriage. While he excluded his wife and attended to his children, his mother and father formed what the patient called "a gruesome twosome." They nurtured each other but abandoned the patient and his sister.

When Mr. AP married his wife, he unconsciously expected her to make up for the maternal deprivation he had suffered as a child. She willingly cooperated, since in her family of origin she had been trained that to be feminine she had to be selfless and to give to others. For a while this was a perfect match between someone who needed to be given to and someone who needed to give. When she became pregnant and felt dependent, however, Mr. AP was not available to her. He was preoccupied with his business, and almost missed being at her delivery. There was a growing resentment that developed in his wife. She had tried so hard to be a good wife, yet her husband did not reciprocate and respond to her needs. She expressed some of her feelings of hurt and unhappiness, but Mr. AP could not understand why she was so emotional.

In a subsequent session, he explored why he could not understand his wife's being emotional. He told me that in his family no one was emotional, except his sister Helen. "Helen was the only one to express her unhappiness, but no one comforted her. Instead, she was ignored or criticized by my parents, as if something was wrong with her for being so upset and emotional." I commented that it seemed that Helen was the one who expressed the underlying emotions and unhappiness for the entire family. The unhappy feelings of both parents seemed to have been split off as unbearable, and projected into Helen, since neither parent had been able to confront their own losses and mourn them. It was as if there was a family taboo against being unhappy, an inability to comfort, and the facade of a happy family was presented to the world. Mr. AP admitted that he felt that "being emotional meant you were weak, fragile, and vulnerable, and that one should have a stiff upper lip. Being unhappy and complaining resulted not in comfort but in being criticized. Being emotional was looked down upon, and I didn't want to be like Helen."

He admitted that he fought against feeling fragile and vulnerable. He said, "I fought hard to make the world appear to be the way I wanted it to be by denying my vulnerability. As a child I was also sensitive, and I was afraid I would not survive. I got little or no protection or guidance from my parents and was afraid I'd crumble and fail. As a child I had to pick myself up and go it alone. I avoid things that I don't do well or am afraid of. I know by not facing my feelings I'm not leading a full life, but then I think of my sister; I see her as a failure. Being emotional means you are fragile and a failure, while being unemotional like my parents means survival and success."

He then spoke about his maternal grandmother, who unlike his mother was nurturing to him. He would spend weekends and holidays with his grandparents, with whom he felt special and experienced love and warmth. It was a happy home; they laughed heartily. When his grandmother died, he felt lost and alone, but did not mourn her loss. Instead, he said, "I blocked all my feelings out. My grandmother had liked being with me, and we had a good time together when she was alive. I recall the intense loneliness I felt. I recall sitting at the dining room table alone, with nobody to go to for comfort or help. I said to myself that I would not let myself become depressed. I picked myself up from the table and said 'never again.'" I asked if he meant that he would not become attached again, so that he would not suffer the loss. He agreed that he defended himself against that, since he was so sensitive and was critical of himself if he became depressed like his sister.

The patient then discussed his anger at his father for not being more emotionally involved. After ventilating his feelings, he recognized that his father was limited by his traumatic life experiences and that economic security was paramount because of his Depression mentality. Mr. AP then proceeded to involve his father in his business decisions, and by sharing this area developed a positive relationship with him. The father was able to affirm the patient, something he had never done during the patient's childhood. The father even admitted that he was not much of a father, having left this responsibility in the hands of his wife.

The patient then worked on his feelings about his mother, recognizing that excluding his wife and being involved with his children was a way of punishing her. He had been deprived of nurturing by his mother, and he displaced his anger onto his wife. He wanted her to make up for the lack of feeling important and cared for by his mother. His wife, however, felt suffocated by his demands. It seemed clear that he denied her separate existence, except as a need-satisfying maternal object. The patient admitted he felt uncomfortable being alone. He associated this with the helplessness and loneliness of his childhood. He recounted a dream. "I was being marched off to a concentration camp to be killed during World War II, and my parents, who were standing together, did nothing. They both just looked on." He never felt safe and protected, especially by his mother. Her alliance was primarily with her husband, since both of them had been traumatized during World War II, and the patient felt lost and abandoned.

He said he had trained himself not to be anxious and depressed, and demeaned his wife when she expressed these feelings. I suggested that I could understand his need to repress these feelings that were threatening to his self-esteem and shameful, and that perhaps he had needed his wife's help to express these feelings for him. But now the conditions of his childhood do not exist, and it is safe for him to express these feelings for himself and to be a more complete person. (I interpreted his projective identification and tied it in with his childhood. I also reframed it in a positive light, so as not to be critical or judgmental. This took his wife out of the scapegoat role, redefined expressing emotions as good, and appealed to his sense of mastery.) He recognized that he did not need to protect himself against being ignored or demeaned by his parents if he expressed his feelings. Gradually, after working this conflict through repeatedly, he became more able to be in touch with how he felt and to be able to verbally express his emotions himself.

He then talked about seeing women as either sexual objects or as if they were genderless, neither man nor woman. As an adolescent he viewed girls only sexually and never developed a friendship with them. He would not initiate a relationship for fear of rejection, but waited until he received some signal that the woman was interested. He did not trust women to be interested in him or to be giving towards him. He said, "I yearned for a woman to protect and nurture me, but I didn't trust them. Certainly that feeling of distrust came from my mother; although I did trust my grandmother, it wasn't the same as my own mother."

He reviewed his previous relationships with women before he married his wife and was aware that he either used them or they had to give up their autonomy to satisfy his demands. His wife was quite young and naive when he met her. He said, "I was smitten when I first laid eyes on her. I feared that she was unapproachable and would reject me, since she seemed so attractive and vivacious." After waiting several months, he called her up for a date, and it went very well. After they were married, she attended to all his needs and he was happy. Things went well until she became pregnant and delivered a baby. He did not satisfy her desire to feel protected and nurtured during this period. She withdrew when he was unable to gratify her neediness. In response he withdrew defensively into his business and their relationship became more and more distant. She then resented "playing third fiddle," since he placed his business first, his children second, and her last.

Subsequently he gained insight into his anger at his wife and mother for not satisfying his needs, and he experienced his wife's neediness, like his mother's, as an abandonment. This was reinforced when she withdrew and lost interest in his business activities. He said, "She wasn't excited any more in what was happening in my business. She's no longer supportive of my efforts. I was planning on going to a meeting out of town and had hoped she would join me there, but she wasn't interested in joining me. I had hoped that, after the meeting, we could spend another day together sightseeing.

"She takes me for granted, and doesn't greet me at the door when I come home. She stays in bed and ignores me. But when our son entered the bedroom and turned on the T.V. and wanted to play with her, she got up and attended to him. I felt less important than my son. Now that I'm talking about it, I wonder if she is doing to me what I did to her, probably out of vengeance." Since he was ready to retaliate again by ignoring her, I suggested another alternative perspective that would not escalate the vendetta: "Maybe that is the case, but I wonder if she wants you to empathize with her, how she felt when you did that to her. Now you can experience what she felt and understand her better."

He then said, "It hurts me to see her depressed and angry." I commented that he did seem to empathize with her. He commented, "I know if I'm not sensitive to her and her needs, if I diminish her self-esteem like my parents did to me, the marriage will not survive. I'm feeling less vulnerable and lonely and can face the fact that time is running out and our marriage is at stake. If she remains unhappy, our relationship is too poisoned and we'll have to dissolve the marriage for her sake and mine. I'm now as hurt as she is. I can feel her hurt now and understand

what you're saying to me. In business I try to do everything correctly and to resolve issues as they come up. I
had not done so in the marriage. We need to face and resolve issues and I have to make her feel important. She is
important to me, and I want a solid marriage. I know
things can't be as exciting as our first meeting, when I was
infatuated with her, but I respect and desire her.

"She still perceives me as putting the business ahead
of her. She complained that when I used to come home,
I'd get on the phone with clients or people at the office. I
got a cellular phone and do my calling of business associ-
ates in the car on the way home. Now, when I come home
I'm there for her. I am trying to change."

I commented, "I understand what you told me about
having to cut yourself off from your feelings and attachments in order to survive when you were growing up. It
was helpful then and adaptive, but it's damaging now and
destructive to your marital relationship. When you can't
feel your own pain, it becomes almost impossible to empathize and feel your wife's pain. Then she feels alone and
unloved, just as you felt when you were growing up, because your mother could not tolerate her own pain to confront and mourn her losses."

He commented that he does feel his own pain now, is
not ashamed of it, and can empathize with his wife's pain.
He had not wanted to be like his sister, who admitted her
pain, but was excluded and scapegoated in his family. He
now realized there was a collusion in his family to deny
pain, and to demean anyone who openly expressed it. He
needed to be connected and to have an intimate relationship with his wife. He no longer dehumanized women as
sexual objects or as protective parental figures to satisfy
his needs. He was breaking out of the "bubble" he had

erected for himself, which was similar to the one his mother had created.

He said he was mourning the loss of not having protective parents during his childhood, and was now in touch with his own and other people's pain. He felt more vital and complete as a person. He said, "I've opened up my eyes to the world, and can see others more clearly. I don't understand it all or feel I can deal with it all yet, but I don't hide my feelings under a rug anymore. I find myself sometimes leaving out things here in the session that are uncomfortable, but I catch myself and try to face them. It's not only in my marriage, but I've had trouble with intimacy in the rest of my relationships. Being able to feel is important to me. Not only can I feel pain but I can feel happiness and joy. It's hurtful, but I feel so much more alive. I had worried that I'd killed my nerve endings and could not feel again. Even other people are looking at me differently. I like the mystery of it and I feel very alive. I'm now running on all my cylinders and I want my wife to be part of that excitement.

"After I express my feelings to her, I hope she understands and that too much damage has not been done and it's not too late. If it is too late, I have to decide what is best for me and go on with my life. It will be painful to have to go through a divorce and leave my kids, but I don't want to settle for being half-alive inside by staying in a loveless marriage. She says she would settle, but that's unacceptable to me. I feel strong and free to know that I feel that way and can say that.

"I don't want to be a statistic, even though I know that half the marriages in the United States end in divorce. I don't want to hurt my kids either, though I know of many people who are divorced and even in a second marriage who maintain good relations with their kids. I had felt it was shameful to get a divorce, but it would be more damaging to the kids if my wife and I stayed married and continued the cold war. Many of the people I know, and their kids, seem to be happy even though they are divorced.

"I don't like the idea of a divorce, and I will make efforts to resolve issues in our marriage, but it takes her willingness to cooperate. If she doesn't, I don't feel trapped, and will not stay in the marriage out of fear or avoidance of pain. I cannot go back into being half-alive. We need to *want* to remain in the marriage and work on it together, and hopefully we can revitalize the marriage."

As therapy progressed, the patient was no longer critical of his wife and became sensitive to her needs. The wife's attitude toward him changed as her husband became more insightful and caring. There was a rekindling of their love for each other, and the prospects of the marriage working out seemed good. Thus, couples therapy was not necessary, since they were able to resolve issues between them themselves. Even if the wife had been too damaged by their relationship, and was unwilling to work on their marriage and to stay together, at least there would have been an end to their hurtful, repetitive cycles of vengeance. He, his wife, and the children would have had a chance for a richer and fuller life instead of enduring chronic hostility and sinking into chronic despair.

## TIPS ON WHAT TO DO AND WHAT TO AVOID

1. Try not to side with the patient against his wife. Her reactions were defensive and in response to his behavior. Their interaction can be dealt with through individual or couples therapy.

2. Try not to side with the wife, who was used by the patient as a need-satisfying object, demeaned, and not seen as a separate individual with needs of her own. Otherwise, the therapist will be experienced by the patient as an abandoning parent, his pathology will be reinforced, and he will stop therapy.

3. Try not to side with the patient against his parents, since the goal is to help him integrate his ambivalence and not to continue to use splitting. After working through his feelings, he can then acknowledge their limitations coming from the traumatic events in their lives. He can mourn the deprivation and loss he suffered in his childhood, and hopefully establish a new empathic relationship with them.

4. Preserving the marriage at all costs does not always mean success, nor divorce signify a failure. This is a decision that the couple needs to make for themselves, and it depends on the cost/benefit balance they experience in the marriage. Remaining in a deadening or conflictual marriage can be more harmful to the spouses and children than a divorce. It is not the divorce itself, but the conflict before and after the divorce that has long-term, damaging effects on the children's personality and functioning. If the divorced spouses can resume their functioning together as responsible parents to their children and not tear them apart by continuing conflict or forcing divided loyalties, long-term studies of children of divorce, such as those of Judith S. Wallerstein and J. B. Kelly (1980), indicate that the children can do well.

# 9
# Legacy of
# an Abandoning Mother

## THE CASE OF MR. AM

Mr. AM was a middle-aged male who was an executive in a large corporation. He had come for therapy because his wife was threatening divorce. She never knew when he would be home from the office at night or on weekends. For example, he would often call to say he would be home for dinner at 7:00 P.M. and arrive at 9:00 P.M. Initially, the family waited for him 30 minutes, and then they ate without him. After repeated disappointments, the family would not wait for him at all and started dinner without him. He was wed to his job. That was his priority, and he was not very much involved with his wife and children. Often business emergencies would arise just when the family was about to go on vacation, and they would have to leave without him or need to make other last-minute arrangements. This left his wife and children feeling less important than his work and angry at him for being unreliable. The family atmosphere was never joyous and relaxed, but always tense and insecure. His wife became increasingly angry at his lack of responsibility and his uninvolvement with her and the children and threatened divorce unless he changed.

Mr. AM seemed quite anxious that his marriage might end in divorce, and said he wanted to work toward improving his relationships at home. He was aware he had neglected his family, placing them in a secondary position to his work. However, he felt they benefited financially from his efforts at being a good breadwinner. He seemed to be a compulsively driven individual, emotionally repressed, who had denied his need for his family.

His relationships were mostly task-oriented and distant, with fairly rigid boundaries between himself and others. His wife's bringing up the possibility of divorce had threatened his defenses, and he felt compelled to come for therapy. He complained that his wife was trying to take control of him by her demands, which he resented. He experienced himself as the hardworking husband who was victimized by his wife. He voiced a good deal of resistance to therapy, and resented feeling coerced to come. Even though he was coming out of superficial compliance with his wife, he seemed mildly motivated and was able to provide me with a good deal of his childhood history.

Mr. AM was brought up primarily by his mother, since his father was also totally preoccupied with being a breadwinner and uninvolved with him or his older brother. As in most traditional families, the mother was invested by the father with a position of power over the boys, while he pursued his outside business activities. Mr. AM's mother had difficulty controlling him, since he was very active and rebellious as a boy. His mother would threaten him with abandonment or being sent away if he did not behave himself. At first, he had felt these were idle threats.

Mother then developed a physical ailment, and the patient was told by both parents that if he upset his mother, she would get sick and have to be hospitalized. Because of this family myth, the boundary between fantasy and reality was blurred. The patient felt guilty over his aggressive and angry feelings, fearing they would make his mother sick and she would leave. Therefore, he repressed his feelings. He felt controlled by his mother's position of power, which was demonstrated by her weakness and threats of becoming sick or abandoning him.

The mother also openly preferred the patient's older brother, Bob. Bob looked and behaved more like her side of the family, while the patient was more like her husband's side. A cold war existed in this family between the parents, but the mother never openly confronted the father. Father was a cold, patriarchal, and absent figure, who felt entitled to exercise power over the family. The mother split off her anger at being neglected and feeling powerless, and transferred the conflict with her husband to her two sons. Her preference for Bob was openly expressed by the mother, who admired Bob and encouraged him to achieve. She showed little interest in and devalued the accomplishments of the patient. Bob became an extension of the mother's frustrated ambition and need for power and self-esteem. Thus Bob felt entitled to feel superior and to bully his younger brother.

During the patient's adolescence, the mother indeed did abandon the patient while he was away at summer camp. Without notifying the patient, she left her husband and took Bob with her to her parents' home, intending to get a divorce. His father notified the patient at camp that the mother had left with Bob. A month later, on the urging of her own parents, the mother relented and returned home with Bob. Things calmed down, but the conflict between the mother and father was never openly expressed or resolved.

I interpreted the defense of projective identification used by his mother. "I suspect your mother also felt abandoned by your father, and perhaps needed to get rid of the way she felt with her husband, that is, inferior, powerless, and insecure, by inducing these feelings in you. I can understand how difficult and confusing it must have been for you then." The patient said he really was not aware of his feelings and never openly expressed any towards his mother or brother. He suspected that his disciplinary problems at school may have been a way of rebelling against his mother without having to confront her.

When the patient seemed engaged in treatment, I interpreted his projective identification with his wife. "It seems that unconsciously you also, like your mother, displaced your feelings of not being important and helpless onto another person, your wife. That may have been your method of mastering the trauma with your mother, doing to your wife what your mother did to you. But now you can be the active one and not the passive victim that you were as a child. Unconsciously you may have needed to make your wife feel less important, insecure, frustrated, and angry, and to have her express these feelings for you." He admitted that he tended to respond to his wife with such behavior, recognizing he was frustrating her and rendering her helpless. (In my mind I questioned whether he was simply being compliant with me also, that possibly this interpretation was premature, since he seemed to intellectualize this insight. Superficial compliance might be his way of protecting his connection with his mother. He could further resist recognizing his split-off angry and sadistic feelings so as to remain a good boy.)

His identification with his father's obsession with work provided him with the rationalization and vehicle for acting out his anger. His father also became the breadwinner while neglecting the role of father. Mr. AM repeated the same role pattern with his wife that had existed between his parents. Being a workaholic and being late was also used by him to repeat his mother's unpredictable and demeaning behavior by keeping his wife dangling in the wind and chronically insecure. He admitted that it was only his wife's threat of divorce that reversed the power equation, leaving him with the underlying fear of abandonment he had as a child with his mother.

The patient discussed the above experiences with his mother and wife, and I empathically suggested that he must have felt it was useless to express his feelings verbally to his parents, since his mother did not seem to be able to see or hear him and his father was absent. The only way open to him, he must have felt, to express himself was through behavior. I said, "I understood how difficult it was for you to acknowledge your feelings, since you felt your mother was biased against you and would not listen, or else it might have resulted in your mother further rejecting you or leaving to be hospitalized. You needed to comply and be a good boy to sustain your relationship with your mother."

He had a dream in which he could not speak and was paralyzed, which he recognized as his need to remain silent with his mother to feel secure and connected to her. His alliance with me developed over a number of months, which permitted him to gradually come out of hiding from behind a compliant false self. After processing and working through his fear of truly being himself, he developed more and more trust in our relationship. He felt safe with me and was able to own and express his angry feelings at me, which he was not able to do with his mother. I contained his anger, did not become defensive, retaliate, or threaten him with abandonment. After testing me, he felt that I heard him and it was safe to express his feelings.

Mr. AM also talked about his competition with his older brother, Bob, whom he had surpassed economically. This was also one of the reasons he worked so hard, hoping to prove to his mother that he was just as good or even better than his brother. (This seemed to me to be a further denial of reality, since his mother was not aware of Mr. AM as a distinct and separate person, but had displaced her anger at her husband onto Mr. AM. However, sublimating his anger into work had proved to be useful and was not self-destructive.) Even though Bob was preferred, he did not establish boundaries between himself and his mother, since she used him as an extension of herself. Bob did not achieve an autonomous true self even though his mother favored him. She was also insensitive to Bob as a separate individual and to what he needed for his own growth. His mother attempted to live vicariously through Bob and his achievements (the depressive family dynamic), and he unconsciously got back at her by being self-defeating and by not fulfilling his potential.

Even though Bob was a failure, the mother never affirmed Mr. AM's successful achievements, and she continued to focus her attention on the older brother. Mr. AM slowly became aware that the reality of his success meant little to the mother, as she was still fighting the battle with her husband and expressing it through her sons. Mr. AM would never really connect with his mother as a genuine and unique person, he realized, and would never get what he wanted from her. He mourned the fact that he would never be acknowledged as a valued son. On the other hand, he changed his childhood picture of her from a cruel and abandoning mother to a more mature view of a helpless and pathetic person. She herself was a constricted, unfulfilled, and deprived person, who could not cope with situations and could never give him what he needed. She also was a victim of her circumstances, just as he was, and he could feel more sympathetic toward her. His need for vengeance diminished gradually, as he differentiated himself from his mother and his wife from his mother. He was then able not to be punishing toward his wife and children.

He recognized that his wife's attending to their boys' needs was appropriate, and she was not his mother, who lavished her attention on his older brother and neglected him. He had also transferred his competition with his brother onto his two sons. Out of his own feeling of neglect and anger, he was insensitive to his wife's needs, and unable to see her for the caring person that she truly was. He recognized that he had perpetuated a pattern that existed in the family of his childhood, and wondered if this might have been true of his father's experience with his own family of origin. He was happy that he had stopped this pattern, and that it would not progress through subsequent generations.

## TIPS ON WHAT TO DO AND WHAT TO AVOID

1. Even though the patient is coerced into coming by his wife and is superficially compliant, it is important to empathically recognize this openly with the patient and to continue to try to establish a working alliance.

2. This patient is also resistant because of split-off, sadistic impulses toward his abandoning mother. Even though he is cut off from his feelings, continued work with him and recognition of why this occurred can slowly help him reown and verbally process these feelings.

3. Once a safe holding environment is established, the patient probably will test the therapist about the safety of verbally expressing anger. It is important to contain the patient's anger at the therapist and not to become defensive, retaliate, or abandon him. To do so would only reinforce his pathology, while not doing so would enable the patient to reown his split-off aggression.

4. It is important for the therapist to avoid becoming judgmental or frustrated. Because of the terrible insecurity and cruelty this patient suffered as a child, he needed to develop a false compliant self in order to sustain contact with his mother and to survive. It is important for the therapist to be patient, since progress will be slow with individuals who have been so repeatedly traumatized during their childhood.

5. The therapist can recognize that this patient was scapegoated by his mother, while his brother was her savior. However, both brothers were traumatized by this splitting. They were responded to not according to what they needed but according to what the mother needed. It is imperative that the therapist be sensitive to the patient's spoken and unspoken needs, and help him develop autonomy and a true self.

# 10

## Legacy of
## an Abandoning Father

## THE CASE OF MR. AF

Mr. AF was a young businessman in his thirties, who came for therapy because he felt he was missing out in life. Many of his friends were getting married, settling down, and having children, but he could not get intimately involved with a girlfriend, seeing women only as sexual objects. He would have only brief sexual affairs without emotional involvement. Now he was experiencing a sense of emptiness, loneliness, and despair, and had come for help. He stated, "I can fuck, but I can't make love to a woman." He was moderately depressed, and used sex and alcohol to escape into oblivion. He fit the diagnosis of a dysphoric character disorder with borderline features.

In obtaining a family history, I found out that his father had been an executive for a large international corporation, and the family had to move around the country a number of times. His father was a workaholic, dedicated to his job and minimally involved with his wife and children. Mr. AF's mother had a difficult time adjusting and integrating into each new community. She was left without an ongoing support system of friends because of having to move around, and she received no emotional backup from her husband's or her family. Both she and her husband were first-generation Americans. The mother's family had come from northern Germany, and the father's family came from southern Italy. Her parents were biased against southern Italians, thinking they were not white, and had disapproved of the marriage. They were judgmental, and distanced themselves from their daughter and son-in-law. They felt she should have married someone from their own nationality, which they considered superior. Her in-laws and husband sensed that they were being discriminated against, and reacted defensively. The husband's parents retaliated by rejecting their new daughter-in-law, leaving the patient's mother to fend for herself.

Mr. AF's father's solution was to move away from both families. The mother had given up her career when she married and assumed the role of a traditional wife. Her husband empowered her to be responsible for parenting, while he was responsible for being the breadwinner. She gave birth to three children, and devoted herself to their care. He was neither supportive of her emotionally nor involved with the children. The patient, Mr. AF, was the middle child, with an older brother and a younger sister. Prior to the patient's adolescence, the mother became depressed and began to drink secretly. When this became obvious to the family, the father's solution was to buy a larger house in a beautiful location. He hoped this would make his wife feel better, and she would stop drinking. In order to earn more to provide for this better lifestyle, he accepted an advancement at work that required him to be away from the family for even longer periods of time.

He consciously rationalized that moving away and giving his wife more material comfort would solve her problems. In addition, he did not want to be intrusive and interfering, as his parents had been with him, and thus avoided dealing with the problem.

This solution, however, was no solution at all; it only made matters worse. He distanced himself all the more and was not available to his wife. Her drinking increased, and eventually she was not able to function any longer as a mother. The patient's older brother left home to go to college, and by default Mr. AF had to assume the role of parent to his mother and younger sister. Mr. AF was aware that his father's abandonment had contributed not only to his mother's decompensation and alcoholism, but also to his being forced to become a surrogate spouse/parent.

This family does not fit neatly into my family diagnostic typology. It appeared that the father's workaholic attitude probably was a reflection of his own unconscious anger at being considered inferior by his wife's family and the alienation from his own family for marrying her. Both families had used distancing to punish the married couple. The father did not confront and attempt to work out a resolution to this conflict, but avoided it himself by becoming distant and obsessed with work. His wife felt hurt by his neglect, decompensated, and the son was forced to take charge of his mother, younger sister, and the running of the home. The family could be subsumed under the borderline/hysterical family typology. The patient complied with the demand to be in a role of surrogate husband and parent, which kept the family together. Mr. AF did all the cooking and cleaning, and looked after his sister. The mother confided some of her despair to the patient and at times when intoxicated was mildly seductive toward him, as if he indeed were her husband.

The patient never confronted his father, but presented a compliant false self. Mr. AF's underlying anger was displaced outside the home, where he stopped studying at school, became a truant, and fell in with a semidelinquent gang. He started smoking marijuana and was arrested for some minor scrapes with the law. His father was called and had to return home to rescue Mr. AF. Here again, the father was not really invested in discovering and working out what was wrong, but accepted Mr. AF's promise that he would be a good boy and not do it again. Clearly these were cries for help by Mr. AF, but his father did not hear them and continued to avoid family problems and to be overinvolved with his work.

Gradually, in treatment, the patient became aware of his intense rage at his father for skipping out of difficult situations and escaping into his work. The father rationalized that he would not be like his in-laws or his own parents and intrude into others' lives. He felt this was the best solution to all problems, giving people the freedom to resolve their issues for themselves.

Indeed, the entire family did not confront anger and conflict, but avoided it and acted out: the father with his workaholic addiction, the mother her alcoholic addiction, and the patient with his semidelinquency and alcohol use. In addition, during adolescence the patient started using sex as another form of addiction, using girls to release his anger and to feel less depressed. He stopped acting out his conflicts with the delinquent subgroup when he switched his addiction to sex, yet he always felt empty and lonely.

His ego boundaries were too closed, and he was too distrustful to feel intimate with another human being. He had no true male buddies and only used women as sexual objects, just as he felt used, neglected, and abused by both his parents. His attitude seemed to be that you thought only of yourself, and you got what you needed.

Gradually in therapy he became aware of his intense rage at his father for not being more involved, which frightened him. His father was getting older and now had a heart condition, and the patient was fearful that he would explode and destroy his father if he vented his repressed anger.

After considerable time working through his anger in therapy, however, he was able to confront his father in a relatively nonhostile way. He asked his father why he had not taken the mother to a hospital where she could dry out and be treated. The father replied that he had tried, but the mother resisted going. Father then gave up and simply left the scene. Mr. AF then told his father that because of the father's inability to deal with his sick wife, the responsibility was dumped on Mr. AF while he was still an adolescent. He said, "I had to pick up the tab for your problems with Mom, and it was too much for me. I felt deserted by you, yet couldn't express my anger, since you were the only stable parent. Mom was falling apart, slowly committing suicide by drinking, and I was helpless to do anything about it. I felt you didn't want to deal with the situation, and that it was useless to turn to you for help."

Because of therapy, the patient had broken the family pattern of avoiding confrontation. Since rejection had not occurred when Mr. AF expressed his honest emotions, his father was also able to reveal himself. The father asked Mr. AF if he could come to therapy to give his perspective, and the patient agreed to several joint sessions with him. Father admitted neglecting his family and apologized to the patient for displacing the family responsibility onto him.

The father said he had come from a poor family, and had heard his parents always fighting over money. His parents had marital difficulties, which they also did not face, but blamed all their problems on lack of money. He had bought into the myth in his parents' family that lack of money was the source of all evil. Thus he felt that if he earned enough money it would cure any marital problem in his own family. He now realized that his view of things, even with his family of origin, was wrong, and avoided the real issues, which became displaced onto the issue of money.

Father also admitted that he became too involved in the rat race at work. He wanted to become CEO of one of the branches of the company, to earn more money and have more prestige. He would prove to his wife's family that he was good enough to have married their "precious" daughter. Ambition and the need to prove his worth were what spurred him on. He admitted he was angry at his wife for being weak and for not holding up her end of the bargain by taking care of the children and being supportive of him.

In the next session with Mr. AF alone, the patient said, "My father is angry at my mother for being weak, but he doesn't see himself. He was weak also. He should have taken charge and hospitalized my mother before she destroyed herself with drink. My mother eventually died of cirrhosis, and he just stood by and watched it happen. He saw she was deteriorating physically and wasn't able to function. Was he getting back at her parents to prove she wasn't such a bargain, and that he was Mr. Success?"

The patient also suspected that the father had had sexual affairs, and that somehow his mother had found out about one of them. He recalled her accusing him of being involved with another woman, and mocking him for being disloyal, but he was not sure if this was accurate or simply part of his mother's paranoid attitude as she deteriorated mentally and physically from her drinking. He realized that his parents' sexual life together clearly must have been poor. He then wondered if he blamed his parents' problems on sex, just as his father had blamed his parents' problems on money.

He said that his goal in therapy was to stop "fucking the world," to get over his anger, and to establish friendly relations with people. His father had been addicted to money, and Mr. AF was addicted to sex. Both these addictions also served as an outlet for anger and a way to gain self-esteem and a sense of power. He also became aware that his father did not want to be intrusive and judgmental, as his own parents had been, and that his father felt that he gave others freedom to be themselves. The patient felt more compassion and forgiveness toward his father, even going so far as to take a vacation together with him. He had felt betrayed and abandoned by his father as well as his older brother because of their lack of involvement and self-centeredness. He then decided that he wanted to form closer friendships with men and to be more social. He seemed to be going through his adolescence, which he had missed, in wanting to be part of a peer group of buddies. This also indicated to me that possibly group therapy could be added at this point.

With women, the patient wanted to integrate his sexuality with tender and loving feelings. Before his mother's deterioration she had been loving and protective. He had been angry at her for neglecting his needs and had been embarrassed by her alcoholism, which further isolated him from his peer group. He began dating, and slowly built up a friendly relationship with a woman, instead of sexual one-night stands, which he referred to as "bim, bam, thank you ma'am." Previously he selfishly got what he needed sexually, and, in anger, abandoned the woman. He had felt used and neglected, and felt justified in using others for his own needs.

He continued in individual therapy and was also placed into group therapy. Initially in group he was guarded and defensive, but gradually opened up and became an active member. The group served as both a surrogate family and the peer group he had never had. He was integrated into the cohesive group structure and learned to care for others, and his needs were responded to and supported by other members. The group thus served as a corrective emotional experience, while he continued to deal with outside relationships in individual therapy.

## TIPS ON WHAT TO DO AND WHAT TO AVOID

1. Establish a safe holding environment that is sensitive to the patient's needs, since he had not felt safe, protected, or responded to in his family of origin.

2. Help the patient become aware of gender stereotypes that constricted his parent's lives and the ethnic bias that was damaging to his parents' family life.

3. Help the patient learn to cope differently than the pattern of avoidance of conflict and distancing that existed in his family.
4. Help the patient become aware of, process, and work through his feelings instead of acting them out through addiction to work, alcohol, or sex.
5. Help the patient not to feel alienated in a family-like setting, which may provide an emotionally corrective experience. Adding group therapy to the individual therapy, a combined approach, is helpful.
6. After the patient can integrate feelings and trust that others will listen and be responsive, conflict can be openly confronted and resolved through verbal dialogue.

# 11

# Conflict in a Modern
# Two-Career Family

## THE CASE OF MR. TC

Mr. TC was a 40-year-old male partner in a law firm, who came for therapy because his marriage seemed to be failing. He stated that he had to slave long hours at work in order to become a partner, and as a consequence his marriage was in trouble. He was alienated from his wife and also from the children. He was fearful that his marriage had deteriorated because of his absence from the family. His wife, Joan, was also a lawyer, but had gone onto the "mommy track" in order to be available to their two children. As a consequence, she did not rack up sufficient billable hours and was not up for promotion to partner in her law firm.

The patient seemed very motivated to work on his problem, and felt hopeful, since his wife was also in therapy. We established a therapeutic contract and our goal was to help him to become more of a person, improve his marriage, and not simply be a slave to his work. The diagnosis was an adjustment reaction to marital conflict.

His boundaries seemed intact and semipermeable. He was a bright and motivated patient, who had previously been in therapy during college and thus was psychologically minded.

His family history was relatively normal. He came from a traditional home, with a father who was the uninvolved workaholic breadwinner. He was an only child, and always felt deprived of his father's attention. There was a mildly seductive relationship with his mother, who focused on her son possibly because she also was deprived of her husband's attention. There was a tradition of male privilege in his home, as well as a model of an uninvolved, distant, workaholic father. He identified with his father, yet felt empty and guilty over his own lack of involvement with his family.

After several months of therapy, the patient reported a dream. He said, "I had a dream yesterday that I was driving in the country to a wedding. My wife Joan tells me she wants me to move out of the house, to leave. I start crying as I see the collapse of my family life. She gives no reason. Am I acting out my guilt in the dream for not being available? In the movie *The Age of Innocence*, Newland Archer suspects that his wife secretly knows he had passionate feelings for Countess Olenska. When I talked last week about a fantasy of having an affair with a female associate at the firm, I felt you minimized it. Yet I feel guilty, like Archer, about the temptation, especially as I now get closer to my wife. We did explore why I considered having an affair. I know I felt impotent and powerless to manage my work load, but now I can control my professional life and be home with Joan and the children. The thought of having an affair made me realize the danger I was in, which I had not wanted to face. Now I have arranged to have a regular work schedule, and my wife and I are closer. We go out together and have fun, and we are re-creating family life. But feelings about having an affair still linger."

In the next session he reported another dream. "I had a dream this morning in which I am on the subway and can't get out. The emergency door is shut and a key is needed to open it up. I use my key to get out at the next station. In my pocket is a child's drawing, like one that my daughter might make. My friend Bill appears and says the drawing was done by one of his kids, and I give it back to him. He says it's a drawing that was done a long time ago. I then awoke with a terrible headache. Nothing improved in Bill's relationship with his wife. He had a long affair, and his marriage went on the rocks. His kids used to draw pictures for him like my daughter. Bill is my alter ego, showing what could happen to me eventually if I had an affair. My work with the firm became too important. I felt trapped in working hard to get my promotion to partner, but I was forgetting my marriage. Now my family and I sit at the dinner table together, and it's wonderful to hear the children's tales about school. I'm taking more of a leadership role, and come home several days a week early to have dinner together."

He discussed these two dreams further. "In the first dream, my wife discovered that I considered cheating and wants to leave. I was the one who minimized the temptation of having the affair, not you, I realize. I was at a point in the relationship with Joan of not feeling passionate with her. We were in a dull situation, going by the demands we both had to satisfy—jobs, kids, and bills. The sheer thrill of anticipating seeing someone and feeling passion was needed, and it didn't occur with my wife. Our relationship is on a different basis now. Previously, I was working late a lot, depressed about the type of life I was leading, having to stay in town in lonely hotel rooms, instead of driving home to the suburbs. I was disappointed that I didn't get the promotion to partner in the firm earlier after all that effort. I didn't feel empowered. When I could excite a woman, it enhanced my self-esteem and sense of masculinity.

"What made it worse was that my wife was angry at me for being away so much and had withdrawn. She has a full-time job also as a lawyer, and expected me to share equally in the responsibilities of the home and children. She was cold, and yelled at me, so I got away from her as a result. I reacted by avoiding her further, by working long hours at the office. I felt trapped by my circumstances and out of control. On weekends she did what she wanted to do and left me with the children. Since she cared for them all week, they were now my responsibility. I had no time for myself to unwind.

"After we talked in therapy, I didn't react by further withdrawal, since I recognized I was helping to create a vicious cycle. The more I withdrew from her anger, the more angry she became, and we were becoming more and more distant from each other. I recognized this would eventually lead to a divorce. I made a deliberate effort to gain control of my work, so I could take more responsibility for the children during the week. I didn't hold onto old patriarchal views but recognized we needed to share the responsibility for the children more equally. My taking the initiative had an impact on Joan. I helped dress and feed the children, and I took them to school in the mornings. Our relationship now flows naturally and more calmly. I hope that I've found the key and can get off that moving train so that our marriage can achieve a better balance."

I asked about his giving Bill back the child's drawing, and what he thought it symbolized. He replied, "When Bill first told me of his divorce, of losing his family and living alone, I remember in the dream giving him a picture to remind him of his family. I was also reminding myself of the richness and tenderness of having a family. It's precious putting my son or daughter to sleep or walking them to school. I didn't want Bill's picture for myself.

"In *The Age of Innocence* Archer's son represents what he couldn't achieve for himself—spontaneity, less constriction. Conforming to be part of a family and community was pitted against individual passion in the movie. I made reservations at a Russian restaurant, since Countess Olenska had been married to a Russian or Polish nobleman. I don't want to choose, I want both the family and the passion, yet it remains an enigma for me. Can I have both?"

I pointed out also the conflict between his individual ambition at work and the needs of his family. He replied, "In my understanding before, I saw myself as helping the family by performing the traditional role of being the breadwinner. So I saw them as being together."

I said that I guessed that was the way it was with his father. He agreed, "Yes, my family was very traditional. He saw himself basically as the provider, and he never changed a diaper nor was very involved with the children. I refused a case that required traveling out of town. I was anxious about setting that limit, but I said that this assignment would not really help me to achieve my objective of being promoted to partner. It haunts me that it took me so long to be considered for partner. In the office culture people talk about it, it's a competitive, macho view.

"In *The Age of Innocence*, Archer was driven by competition for social acceptance and prestige. In our culture, it's how fast you can make your first million. You can become constricted by going along with the social values around you. At my firm, so few have an investment in their family. They're single, or divorced, or uninvolved. It's empty and materialistic. I value what I have in the family. The partner I work with sees himself primarily as a breadwinner, and his wife brings up the children. I'm not attracted by that traditional patriarchal view. I find family life precious, and enjoy it and appreciate it. I want to have my cake and eat it too—to have both. Junior people at work look at me as a model, since I value my family and do a good job."

In the next session he reported, "We visited my wife's family over the weekend, and while driving back she mentioned that she had not been happy with the marriage. She said couples stay together because of the children. I let it go. I then called her at work today to see how she was doing. She told me yesterday when she came home that she was angry at my not being in the house at the beginning of the year, because I worked such long hours. I brought up our going on a trip together next weekend, just the two of us to get close again. She said that she didn't know if that was possible, since there is no one to leave the kids with over the weekend."

I asked, "Do you think that her excuse was accurate or is she avoiding you, not trusting that you will be different?" He said, "I don't know. She expects something from me to change before she opens up and trusts me. Last week I took her to the Russian restaurant and a show, and she was happy after that. There's a distance between us, and she expects me to make the first steps and to continue being considerate of her needs. I have to take steps to get closer and just keep hanging in there.

"I rented a movie over the weekend, *The Story of Camille Claudel*. It was about the sculptress who had a relationship with Auguste Rodin. He had a surge of artistic creativity because of her. When Joan and I were both in law school we were helpful to each other, and were both more productive."

I asked if Camille also became creative. He replied, "No. It was a tragic story. She sacrificed herself for him, and didn't continue her work. It was the opposite of Dashiell Hammett and Lillian Hellman, where she blossomed and he went downhill. Joan feels she has to sacrifice her legal career, since she is a woman and more bonded to the children. In renting the movie, I wanted to prompt a discussion, and I wanted to recognize her position, to agree that she was right. I wanted to say I understood what she is going through. I didn't tell her that directly."

I said, "Then how would she know that was your intention without verbalizing it?" He replied, "I should have validated the female role of Camille Claudel, who was the inspirational muse for Rodin. She was his mistress, despite his having a wife and family. Rodin refuses to leave his wife when Camille asks him to do so. She ends up being committed to an institution. In her childhood, Camille's father was supportive, but he was absent, seeing her only once a week. Her mother was dictatorial and more attached to her brother, Paul. She supported the son, but Camille was the target of criticism from her mother. She escaped feeling controlled by her mother through her relationship with Rodin, but she was too compliant to Rodin, lost herself and never became a full-fledged artist on her own. When Rodin refused to leave his wife, she became unstable emotionally. Her brother, Paul, a conservative guy, put her into an institution. I'm expressing my conflict through the story. She felt exploited by Rodin and developed a paranoia. It was turn-of-the-century Paris, and she believed that Rodin, who was a conservative sculptor, was preventing her from doing her avant-garde work. He was putting obstacles in her path, she believed, that prevented her from becoming a sculptor in her own right. I felt the movie had three themes: one, the feminine role is too compliant and self-sacrificing, resulting in females being exploited by the male; two, her father relinquished his patriarchal role to the mother and did not protect his daughter, which sounds similar to my father who was absent and did not protect me from my authoritarian mother; and three, there was an oedipal theme, with the mother both supportive and seductive with her son, which sounds familiar to my situation also, since my mother turned to me when my father was emotionally absent for her."

In the next session, he reported, "I recalled when my wife and I graduated law school, we both were top students and ambitious about our careers. We both started in different prestigious law firms, but then we had two children. I continued on the path to become a partner, and Joan put her career on hold, since she assumed most of the responsibility for the children. I simply considered it my right as a man to continue my career and to be the protective breadwinner. She felt I exploited her because she was a woman. She wanted me to take an equal share of the responsibility for the kids. Recently I've taken a more equal share of responsibility with the kids, and we have been feeling closer.

"Last night I had to go back to the firm to prepare a brief. She was understanding and did not become angry and withdraw into silence. My activity at home broke the vicious circle that had existed for so long. It felt good. I have to control things at work so they don't get out of hand. I recognize that the pace is growing again with new cases coming in, but I need to preserve my family relationships. Joan and I agreed to go out together for dinner every Friday evening."

I said, "I guess you're saying you don't want Joan to be Camille Claudel to your Rodin. He replied, "Yes, we're sharing more, and I'm sensitive to her needs also. I'm not exploiting her for my career and forcing a constricted and compliant role on her. We are closer. I hate it when we're distant and not talking to each other. I respond better and am less defensive when she says something critical, since I don't feel guilty now. I can't take her for granted. It takes work. I need to be sensitive to her as a person, aware of her needs as well as my own, and to compromise to keep our love alive.

"This week I plan to take her to another restaurant. She likes surprises, and for me to be considerate and romantic. I plan to celebrate her thirty-fifth birthday by arranging a party. How long will I keep coming to see you? Will my life continue to be a roller coaster, with ups and downs? The interest in that other woman helped me to face the issues with my wife, not to avoid them, and to work them through. But that's over. I hope my relationship with Joan becomes stable, that what I'm doing now works, and that it's not too late."

Fortunately, it was not too late, and through his efforts, and his wife also working on the marriage in her own therapy, the marriage was saved. After a year, I received a report that all was going well, that they had made it.

## TIPS ON WHAT TO DO AND WHAT TO AVOID

1. With a motivated patient like this one, don't get in the way of his efforts to improve his self-esteem and his marriage.
2. Help the patient avoid defensive interaction, which is destructive (as when his wife was angry at him for being absent), and to stop confounding matters all the more by his withdrawing.
3. Help the patient become aware of his own father hunger and to realize that the traditional role his father pursued resulted in the patient's and his mother's emotional deprivation.
4. Help the patient become aware that his feeling impotent at work and rejected by his wife contributed to his fantasizing about an affair to bolster his masculinity.
5. Help the patient become aware that the male role has changed, especially in two-career families, and that he need not simply follow in the footsteps of his father or other patriarchal male figures.

# 12

# The Narcissistic
# Borderline Couple

## THE CASE OF MR. AND MS. NB

The marriage of a man with a narcissistic personality disorder to a woman with a borderline personality disorder represents one of the most frequent types of dysfunctional couples coming for marital therapy. This type of couple seems to represent an exaggerated caricature of the traditional cultural gender stereotypes. Many couples who do not suffer personality disorders still demonstrate many of the characteristics of the narcissistic/borderline couple. Familiarity with the interaction and treatment of the narcissistic/borderline couple finds applications with a wider range of apparently normal couples.

## CULTURAL GENDER STEREOTYPES AND PATHOLOGY

The cultural stereotype splits personality traits according to gender, defining men as autonomous, rational, strong, and somewhat obsessional while women are por-

trayed as dependently connected, emotional, weak, and
somewhat hysterical. Although less so now than in the
Victorian era, the culture imposes roles on each gender,
no matter what the inborn temperament or endowment
is for each individual. In addition, as mentioned previously, the rearing of boys solely by their mothers also fos-
ters obsessional/narcissistic traits because of the need to
separate and achieve a male gender identity. The result
of this splitting of personality traits between the genders
that occurred in traditional society was that men and
women needed to enter into a symbiotic relationship to
achieve wholeness. External controls were imposed on
each gender, especially upon women, that constricted the
degree of personal autonomy. The goals of therapy are
to help the couple achieve a greater degree of personal
autonomy, establish a more intimate and supportive
relationship, and integrate so-called "masculine" and
"feminine" traits within each person.

Although the cause of these personality disorders does
not originate with the stereotype, it is in all likelihood
shaped by the culture. When the culture is stable and both
genders are relatively normal psychologically, the stereotyped role functioning can be complementary and adaptive. In its pathological form, as demonstrated by the
narcissistic/borderline couple, the symbiotic relationship
established to achieve wholeness of the self eventually
fails. These couples come for therapy when the symbiosis
is no longer functional, and they interact in a mutually
defeating, defensive manner. They are still dependent on
external confirmation of their self-esteem and personality integrity. Thus, they make efforts to control, manipulate, or punish the other, hoping to gain compliance to the
demands that they impose on their spouses.

## FAMILY STUDIES

In my family studies at New York University Medical Center (Slipp 1988), I noted that there were certain family developmental factors that seemed to be prevalent during the childhoods of individuals suffering from these two personality disorders. This work was done with families containing a borderline child as well as with narcissistic/borderline couples in treatment. In the latter instance, this was based on adult descriptions of their childhoods as related in therapy, which was subject to retrospective distortion, yet we still found repetitious patterns of family relationships. The family dynamics findings were correlational and not causative. Clearly the family, which transmits cultural values to its younger members, was influenced by the culture. Traumatic events and interference with early childhood development, as noted by psychoanalytic observations, may also establish neural pathways in the brain. Biological factors undoubtedly play a significant role, even more so in borderline personality disorders. For a more complete description of the developmental family patterns that were found to be involved, the reader is referred to my book *The Technique and Practice of Object Relations Family Therapy* (Slipp 1988).

### Borderline Personality Disorders

In summary again, there was found to be a pattern and sequence of events in these families of origin that was related to the development of borderline personality disorders in women. Their fathers were noted to be highly narcissistic, demanding continuous admiration from others as external confirmation of their self-worth, and not attending to their wives' needs. As a result, their wives refused to submit to the imposition of being used primarily as a need-satisfying object to bolster their husbands' male egos. When the husbands were unable to control their wives and obtain a sense of wholeness and self-esteem from the interpersonal relationship, they felt helpless and enraged. The husbands then employed the defense of splitting, seeing their wives as bad maternal objects and rejecting them. In response, the wives withdrew, abandoning their nurturing role as a wife and mother, but did not leave the marriage. The fathers then turned to their daughters and seductively bound them to bolster their own self-esteem.

Kernberg (1976, 1986) noted that these daughters, deprived of maternal nurturance and having oedipal strivings, had an early, intense oedipal relationship with their fathers, who served as surrogate mother as well. At times, actual physical seductions by the fathers occurred, as noted by Stone (1981) and Van der Kolk (1986). Our work, however, indicated the seduction need not be physical but could be psychological, which was damaging as well. The daughters won an oedipal triumph over their mothers, and thus fantasies were not differentiated from reality. The result was that boundaries were not established by the father, and the daughters suffered poor impulse control. Later on, the fathers rejected their daughters, and turned to other women to satisfy their narcissistic need for external admiration.

The patients destined to be borderline thus fell permanently from grace, feeling rejected and abandoned by their fathers. The daughters' own developmental needs were ignored, as they complied to the demands imposed upon them by their fathers. The daughters were seduced and abandoned for their fathers' needs. Since their relationships with their mothers were distant and not nurturant, the daughters' self-esteem rested primarily on the relationships with their fathers. The daughters internalized this paternal relationship and experienced themselves as worthless. These women tended to be self-destructive, since they were discarded like rubbish by their fathers. Michael Stone (1988) termed this pattern the *Marilyn Monroe Syndrome.*

Like their fathers, the borderline patients as adults tend to use seductive means to obtain dependency gratification and to enhance their self-esteem. They may also have a repetition compulsion to repeat their childhood experiences by picking narcissistic men like their fathers, who again use and reject them. Thus, a mutually exploitative relationship is established between the woman with a borderline personality disorder and a man with a narcissistic personality disorder, with each feeding off the other to enhance his or her damaged self-esteem.

## Narcissistic Personality Disorders

It was repeatedly found in our clinical case material with men suffering a narcissistic personality disorder that these patients as children were alternately idealized and demeaned. Most of our cases were men, since this disorder seems to be more prevalent with males. This alternating pattern was internalized into the personality, and later found expression as adults in their relations with others.

One common pattern was that the boy was seductively bound by his mother and used as a *surrogate spouse.* This oedipal victory enhanced his grandiosity. However, this role repeatedly alternated with being *scapegoated* by the mother, and the boy then felt demeaned. These men were often phallic narcissists, seducing and abandoning women. Their sexuality became combined with anger, so that sex was used to control and demean women. This repeated the alternating seduction and scapegoating that they experienced as a child. In addition, a seductive borderline woman, like the mother, was found to be an attractive target for these men as adults.

There were several other variants of this pattern of being alternately idealized and demeaned during childhood. One of the most common ones, which I have termed the *Solomon Child Syndrome* (Slipp 1988), occurred when a civil war existed between the parents, who competed for the boy's preference. If the boy sided with and satisfied the demands of one parent, he was idealized by that parent, but this resulted in his being demeaned by the other parent, who saw the boy as a traitor who joined the other side. This pattern was frequently noted in parents who were on the verge of or had completed a divorce and remained hostile to each other. The boy was torn apart by conflicting loyalties, trapped by the imposed demands of one parent and used to punish the other parent. These narcissistic men had difficulty making decisions and commitments, and were also distrustful and cynical about intimate relationships.

Another less frequently found pattern was the *emotional orphan,* who was emotionally abandoned by both parents. These parents were frequently a "gruesome twosome," often very wealthy or upper-middle class, who nurtured each other but not their children. Another person, often a maid or another relative, idealized the boy. These narcissistic men as adults were often distant, cut off from their emotions, and more obsessional.

The result in all these instances was that the patient internalized both an idealized and a demeaned self-image. They then repeated these internalized relationships, and they did to others what had been done to them. They projected this internalized relationship by alternately idealizing and demeaning others. Just as in the Greek myth, Narcissus was looking for mirroring and needed an Echo, who was not seen as a separate person but remained undifferentiated from himself. Echo had to repeat the words he needed to hear to nurture his diminished self-esteem.

## The Personality-Disordered Couple

Both these personality-disordered individuals repeat in their adult relationships the experiences that they had as children. The male with narcissistic personality disorder, who is usually obsessional and repressed, experiences the female with borderline personality disorder, who is emotionally labile, as exciting. She is able to express his repressed emotions, and he can feel alive by vicariously living through her. The female with borderline personality disorder experiences the male with narcissistic personality disorder as the strong silent type, who will calm and contain her emotionality. After the infatuation and honeymoon are over, however, and as they attempt to establish a more permanent equilibrium, problems arise that they cannot resolve.

Both partners have come from homes that have not been sensitive to their developmental needs. They distrust that others will be responsive to them and believe that they need to control the other to obtain nurturance. They both have a poor self-image, and experience frustrations personally affecting their self-esteem. Each is driven by his or her unfulfilled needs because of past deficits, and thus each is also unable to be responsive to the other. The result is ongoing conflict, since neither finds in the other what he or she hoped to find. Through withholding, manipulation, threats, or superficial compliance, they both try to extract what they need in this mutually exploitative relationship. Often a stalemate occurs in their relationship as each resists being coerced by the other. This can result in violence, suicide, separation, or, with more healthy couples, coming for therapy.

## BEGINNING TREATMENT— THE FRAME AND ENGAGEMENT

Treatment is difficult, since both experience themselves as victims of the other, and do not see their shares of the responsibility for the problem. With this externalization of the problem, they both want the therapist to side with them and to force the other to change. They wish to repeat the same form of coercion in treatment that they exercise with each other at home. The therapist needs to set boundaries, and cannot assume the role of judge and side with one party or blame the other. Blaming would only perpetuate the problem, since it can never be mutually acceptable. The therapist can explain that if he or she sided with one partner, the other would object, and therapy would arrive at the same stalemate that has already occurred at home. This has not worked, so repeating this pattern in therapy would be fruitless. The therapist needs to make it clear that usually no one is to blame, and that everyone needs to work together on improving the relationship between them. By hearing from each of the parties, the therapist can help the couple resolve their issues in a different manner than in the past. This will require their willingness to give up the search for blame, which only leads to defensive battles, and to try working together.

To accomplish this task, the therapist needs to take a neutral stance, and to listen to and understand each of the couple's perspectives. During the initial phases of treatment, the therapist has to set the framework and establish a contract and goals. The time, place, fee, and procedures of therapy are outlined. The therapist can stress that it is important for the couple to try to be as open and honest as possible, to bring up issues that trouble them, to listen to the other and try to understand what they are expressing, and not to interrupt each other. There may be times when they feel frustrated, but it is important to express these feelings and to continue to work on the problems in therapy. This sets the boundaries of therapy and establishes how therapy will proceed.

Since men are often the ones who are more resistant to therapy, the therapist needs to address masculine issues to ensure the man continuing in therapy. This can be helped by universalizing this resistance as encompassing many men, empathically recognizing the feelings of the man, and thus creating a safe space for him to bring it up for open discussion. The therapist needs to acknowledge that many men are reluctant to come for help, since they may see this as a personal failure and perhaps a threat to their manhood. The therapist can discuss traditional male cultural stereotypes, which have in the past defined masculine behavior, such as the cowboy or the action hero, who doesn't talk but keeps things to himself, has to be master of all situations alone without help, and always has to be in control. This was part of the socialization that most men learned as youngsters in their families, and from movies, comic books, and society. These stereotypes, however, are changing, since they no longer fit current society, which is also rapidly changing. The therapist can help further by universalizing that, in our current society, male identity is less constricted by these traditional stereotypes and now has a wider range.

The therapist can encourage the man to engage in the process of couples therapy by reframing his participation in therapy in a positive light. The therapist can affirm that by facing a problem and working at it together, the couple hopefully will be able to resolve it themselves. The couple will then learn to master and better deal with situations themselves. The therapist can offer guidance to facilitate their working out conflictual issues, but it remains for them to resolve it satisfactorily between them through continued dialogue.

## Early Treatment Issues

Uncovering the man's repressed feelings early in therapy is not indicated, since feelings are often associated with not being manly or losing status. Once the couple is firmly engaged in treatment, the therapist needs to help them each see their responsibility in the situation, how they feel, how they express or act out these feelings, and how each affects the other. Often a man may experience his spouse as accusing or blaming when she expresses her feelings. When this occurs the man may become defensive, try to justify himself, blame his spouse, attack, or withdraw. Then the spouse feels that she has not been heard, her autonomy is attacked as her husband tries to impose his view on her, and she may feel it is hopeless to communicate. The wife may withdraw or superficially comply, which only fuels the husband's anger even more, resulting in a greater attack. These circular interactional defensive patterns need to be pointed out as self-defeating and only escalating conflicts.

## Middle and Ending Treatment Issues

In the middle phase of treatment, the therapist can help the couple to integrate their splitting, to stop using projective identification, and to reown aspects of themselves placed into the other. Once this is accomplished, both partners can then process their feelings, and have insight into where these feelings come from and how they have dealt with them in the past. Then they can make efforts to resolve issues differently, without self-defeating acting out. Once they have greater awareness and containment of their feelings, they can make efforts to deal with them symbolically on a verbal level. Individually working through these internalized issues is a repetitious task that seems to be necessary to establish new neural pathways that anchor permanent change.

## MR. NP AND MS. BP—AN EXAMPLE OF
## COUPLES THERAPY

A man, Mr. NP, in his mid-forties, and a woman, Ms. BP, in her mid-thirties, came for therapy to improve their relationship, which was foundering. They informed me that this was the second marriage for each of them. The wife worked as a commercial artist and the husband owned his own business. They said they had been married for five years, and that considerable conflict arose over how the husband handled his son and daughter from his first marriage. His wife felt that he was too lenient with them, and was overly generous financially with his first wife. The wife said that her husband had not wanted children in this second marriage, since he felt he had "paid his dues raising his two children and wanted to be free to enjoy life." She said that he wanted a younger, "trophy" wife, with whom he could have fun. After marriage, the wife insisted that she wanted a baby, and after considerable conflict between them they had a child of their own.

In obtaining a family history from each, the husband, Mr. NP, revealed that he came from a wealthy, traditional New England family, in which the father was the domineering patriarch and the mother was submissive to his will. She was concerned about her husband's needs, and relegated the upbringing of her son to a succession of nannies. His father was successful in his own business and prominent in the town in which they lived. The father was active in the church and country club, and had even held political office. Mr. NP said he did not have a close relationship with either parent when he grew up, but felt it was a normal childhood, like other families and without any problems. He also commented that he was admired by his maternal grandparents, who idealized him and made him feel special. He was also generally popular in school and did well academically. Just before he graduated from high school, his father's business became bankrupt. His father, a prominent citizen in the community, felt humiliated by his business failure, and too ashamed to remain in the town. Father, without consulting anyone in the family, put their house up for sale and suddenly moved the family to another state.

Mr. NP said he had to leave high school at the beginning of his senior year, while he was being considered for several prestigious Ivy League universities. The father offered no explanation to his son of why the family had to move at such an inopportune time. His mother simply acquiesced and was supportive of her husband and did not attend to her son's distress. The son was not asked about how he felt about the move, but simply was expected to follow his father's directions without question.

Mr. NP said he had difficulty adjusting to the new high school and did poorly academically. Clearly, he must have been depressed, but I did not question him about his emotions this early in treatment. He then said that he dropped his applications to the colleges, since there was no money for tuition, and worked for several years as a common laborer on construction jobs. His wife commented that he must have been very angry at his parents, but he said he was unaware of any angry feelings toward his parents, even though he took a job that was far below his abilities. His parents never questioned this decision, but accepted it without comment.

After several years, he said, he applied to the state college and was accepted. He graduated with honors and took a job with a large corporation. He then worked his way

up the corporate ladder until he decided to establish his
own business. He had little to do with his parents, not even
inviting them to his first marriage. He had not wanted to
make a commitment to his first wife, but she became pregnant and her family pressured him into marriage. He
submitted to their coercion and married her. A year after
the birth of their child, Mr. NP and his first wife had another child, but Mr. NP was emotionally uninvolved with
his wife and she later obtained a divorce. After a number
of years he met his current wife, who was fifteen years
younger than he, and was a promising artist.

Ms. BP came from a midwestern family, in which her
father was emotionally overinvolved with her and alienated from his wife. They would spend considerable time
together and enjoyed intimate conversations and sports
activities that excluded the mother. She felt special with
her father, who was her "hero" and who seemed to prefer
her to his wife. However, a son was born and the father's
interest shifted over to his son, with Ms. BP feeling permanently diminished and abandoned by her father. He
also established an ongoing affair with another woman
that the patient knew about.

Ms. BP rebelled by becoming a hippie, much to the
embarrassment of her middle-class, traditional family.
Her father became further alienated and her mother also
rejected her because of her lifestyle. She said that her
mother told her, "I don't have a daughter anymore." She
then married an immigrant blue-collar worker, which
further disappointed the family. She was consciously
aware of her anger at her family and knew her lifestyle
and marriage were hurtful to them. That marriage lasted
four years, and there were no children.

She completed art school during those years, and gradually made a name for herself as a serious painter. After her divorce, she said, she was able to support herself with her artwork. She admitted, however, that she had had a problem with alcohol and marijuana. She met Mr. NP at a party, and she was impressed by his "quiet strength." He liked her emotional liveliness and her "uninhibited bohemian nature." They dated for about a year, but Mr. NP again did not want to make a commitment to marriage. She did not simply want to be a "toy or plaything," she said, and manipulated him into marrying her by threatening suicide. He considered her threat serious, was dependent on her and did not want to lose her. He submitted reluctantly to her threat and entered the marriage, but Ms. BP continued to resent the fact that he did not want to enter into a permanent relationship and that she had had to pressure him to marry her. Her old feelings of being seduced and abandoned, of feeling worthless, were probably revived.

She said that she continued to have an alcohol problem in the early days of the marriage, but felt it was more under control now. After several years of marriage, she had to pressure her husband again to get what she wanted—having a child. She threatened to leave him and had several alcoholic binges, where she became physically violent.

He quietly submitted again and did not show any open resentment at having a child, similar to his lack of reaction to being manipulated initially into the marriage, but Mr. NP unconsciously acted out his anger at being coerced by witholding money and sex and withdrawing emotionally, without taking responsibility for it.

There seemed to be a repetitious pattern of submitting to coercion, just as he had done with his father and with his first marriage. He gave in, but then withheld gratifying their expectations. He increased his child support payments to his ex-wife more than was required legally in his divorce agreement. This provoked Ms. BP's anger, since she was concerned that they would not save enough money to ensure the education of their own child. Despite being generous with his children from his first marriage, Mr. NP held tight reins on the money spent in his current marriage. Ms. BP resented the imposed monetary restraints on her, since she had to operate on a tight budget to make ends meet. Mr. NP also began to suffer premature ejaculation, thus not only witholding money but also sexual pleasure from his wife. Conflict between the two then escalated.

To add salt to the wound, Mr. NP bought expensive presents for his children from his first marriage. He also was overly indulgent emotionally, and did not set limits with them. Ms. BP complained that when she had to set limits with them, it put her into the role of the "wicked stepmother" in their eyes, while her husband was the generous "Mr. Good Guy." Ms. BP reacted to her husband's involvement with his children with intense anger and suicidal depression, and began drinking heavily again. When Ms. BP attempted to set limits with Mr. NP's children, he blamed her for causing trouble in his relationships with them. She felt he was spoiling them by over-indulging them with expensive gifts. He felt she was unreasonable and out of control.

Later in therapy, Mr. NP became aware that he was acting out his anger for submitting to her coercion. The repetitious pattern was pointed out of his feeling forced to submit to his father, his first wife, and now his second

wife. Ms. BP was also unaware of the effect of her manipulation to get what she wanted, which had produced anger
in her husband. She only experienced his withholding as
another abandonment. She thought that he was either still
in love or emotionally involved with his ex-wife and preferred her. Secondly, she thought he felt guilty over the
divorce and leaving his children and thus was indulging
them with money at her expense.

Although the couple initially was unaware of their distrustful and hostile interaction, it became clear that the
husband was reacting to his wife as if she were his arbitrary and controlling father. She then became aware that
she felt displaced by her husband's children, and felt less
important than them in his eyes. She complained that she
felt like a second-class citizen, with her husband putting
his children before her. When I asked Ms. BP if she had
ever felt this way before, she insightfully recognized that
it represented a replay of what had happened when her
father turned from preferring her to favoring her younger
brother.

Unconsciously, this couple had selected each other to
replay old scenarios from their childhood. Ms. BP was able
to express Mr. NP's emotions, especially his murderous
rage at his father, which he had repressed from conscious
awareness. He had always felt neglected by his father, who
was involved in his work and was an arbitrary patriarchal
figure. Mr. NP did not even recognize that his working as
a laborer, after the father moved the family to another
state, was his passive-aggressive way of getting back at
and punishing his father. He admitted that he had hoped
to provoke his father and make him feel guilty; he recognized, however, that it did not seem to work—his father
did not feel guilty or even overtly disturbed by Mr. NP's

acting out. His father rationalized his son's working as a laborer as teaching him to be a real man. The father said. he himself had to be tough to succeed and his son needed to endure frustrations, master situations, and learn to be independent—it was good for his character.

Mr. NP intuitively became aware of his wife's Achilles heel, her feeling seduced and abandoned by her father. Thus, he knew exactly where her jugular was, and was able to punish her without taking responsibility for his actions. She felt that if she did not coerce Mr. NP into marrying her or later having a child, he would have remained insensitive to her needs just as her father was during her childhood. She distrusted all men, since she saw them as selfish and as users. Mr. NP also did not trust anyone to be sensitive to his needs and, feeling that he would not be heard, had repressed his feelings.

Although Mr. NP's feelings were not dealt with initially, eventually the interpretation was made that as a child he had had to repress his anger and frustration, since he had felt his father would not listen to him anyway. Thus, he needed the help of his wife to express these angry feelings for him. Now that he was aware of his anger, however, he no longer would need her help and could express them himself. Mr. NP said, "In my family feelings were suppressed, you had to have a stiff upper lip and not complain. Also, my mother never complained, but silently went along with her husband. She was no model of confrontation when there was a conflict, nor could I expect support from her." He did not trust anyone to listen to his feelings and support him, and expressing anger would only lead to further condemnation and rejection. He also felt sorry for his father, he said, and consciously did not want to hurt him.

Ms. BP's support of his entitlement to feel angry at his father facilitated his awareness of his own anger and ambivalence at his arbitrary father. He was further wounded that his father did not seem disturbed that Mr. NP gave up wanting to go to college. In viewing it now as an adult, Mr. NP thought not only was he unconsciously punishing his father, but he also made it easier for his father not to feel guilty about not having money to send him to a private Ivy League college.

Mr. NP then became aware of feeling that he had to do what his wife wanted without having a voice in the decision, just as had occurred with his father. He was angry at her as well. He felt manipulated by her, feeling he had no choice in getting married or having a child. His wife, however, pointed out that it was his withholding a decision and his insensitivity to her feelings that provoked her to try to control him. She felt he induced her into being like his father, and even when she made a simple request, he felt as if he had to comply and had no choice. She said, "He then feels victimized and angry." He realized that a good deal of the restriction on his freedom was self-imposed, and was learned behavior from his childhood. The continued working through of this symbiotic relationship was eventually successful, resulting in greater autonomy for both of them.

## TIPS ON WHAT TO DO AND WHAT TO AVOID

1. Avoid being induced into being a judge, who decides who is the victim and who the criminal. This only perpetuates the splitting and projective identification.

2. Avoid being induced into seeing the borderline as out of control and siding with the reasonable and rational narcissistic person.

3. Avoid siding with the borderline, who may be treated cruelly by the obsessional narcissistic person, as victim.

4. By listening and empathizing with each of the spouses' perspectives, the therapist serves as a model to reduce egocentricity and increase empathic understanding.

5. Clarify how each of the spouses affects and is affected in their interaction, especially how each spouse's need to blame the other and defend against attack may escalate conflict and be self-defeating.

6. Help them become aware of old baggage they are still carrying from their childhood, and how it affects their current relationship.

7. Eventually, interpret their need to use projective identification to deal with split-off aspects of themselves. Reframing this in a positive light and connecting it to childhood experiences is helpful.

# Summary

## FIN-DE-SIÈCLE MENTALITY

It is important for a therapist working with men to become aware of the cultural context that influences male attitudes and behavior. As we come to the end of the twentieth century, there are certain emotional reactions expressed, which are similar to those at the end of the nineteenth century. What I would call a fin-de-siècle mentality comes into existence. The significant aspect in common at the turn of both centuries is that endings remind us of old age and death. Just as an individual's life comes to an end, the culture seems to undergo a death-and-rebirth phenomenon.

The ending of each year is symbolized by the death of feeble old Father Time and the birth of an energetic New Year's baby, as if parental authority has grown weak and is distrusted, since it is no longer nourishing and guiding. Whereas the year-end symbolism has more individual significance, the end of the century (and, even more so, the end of the millennium) is reflected in the wider culture.

Karl Schorske (1981) noted that in fin-de-siècle Vienna the "culture makers in the city of Freud" saw themselves in a "collective oedipal revolt" (p. xxvi). Schorske notes, however, that the revolt of the younger generation was more against "the paternal culture that was their inheritance" and was an assertive search for new meaning. The cohesive fabric of society then seemed to be disintegrating as it does today, leaving men insecure and needing to establish new meaning and hope. This was accomplished by the "dancing stars" that Nietsche spoke about, who arose to the challenge. There were remarkable advances in art, architecture, music, philosophy, psychology, and science, but destructive political forces that arose exploited the insecurity of the masses and eventually led to World War II.

## SYMBIOTIC SURVIVAL OR ANARCHIC INDIVIDUALISM

Some of the same issues that produced the identity crisis for nineteenth-century culture exist today. There also was an end to the previous economic foundation of society and a need to cope with the new technological revolution. In the nineteenth century the Industrial Revolution was born, and in the twentieth century the Postindustrial Revolution occurred. The steam and internal combustion engines have been replaced by computer technology, which further reduced the need for manual labor. It is no longer muscle and sweat that sustain the economy but technical knowledge.

Thus many men in both the nineteenth and twentieth centuries found their existing skills to be no longer of value

in a rapidly changing society. The older values of masculinity that men inherited from their fathers, which emphasized physical strength, became no longer adaptive.
The advancing technology reduced the need for manpower,
displacing men then as it does now. Technical knowledge,
which can be acquired by women as well as men, is what
is needed in today's world. Unfortunately, men have been
falling behind women in educational achievement. Women
are now earning more than half of the bachelor's and
master's degrees at universities.

Many middle-class men have experienced a loss of economic security and feel powerless. They are not protected
by companies who no longer hire them for a lifetime job
or career with yearly increases in salary. Many companies themselves are struggling to survive being threatened
by foreign competition, and need to restrict their work
force and make them work harder. With the weakening
of unions, many blue-collar workers also feel at the mercy
of their employers. Many men, having difficulty fulfilling
the breadwinner role, are also threatened by the loss of
privilege in the home.

Men have reacted in several ways to this identity crisis. Among some men there has been a regression to a
symbiotic survival pattern, with a breakdown of individual
boundaries and a merging into a group for support. These
men feel helpless and victimized by the loss of economic
security, which is accompanied by women and minorities
also competing for the already limited number of jobs.
By finding a scapegoat to attack, group solidarity and
strength is enhanced. Even though this simplistic and
paranoid solution of demonizing another does not address
the real causes for their powerlessness and insecurity, an
illusion of mastery is achieved. The individuals in the

group feel they are doing something and experience themselves less as passive victims at the mercy of others.

For other men a revolt against all paternal authority may result in anarchic individualism. Historically, this latter response was reflected in the nineteenth century by a revolt against rational Enlightenment thinking by philsophers such as Nietzsche and Schopenhauer, who emphasized irrationalism, subjectivism, and emotionality. In the twentieth century, the postmodernist revolt by Foucault and Saussure declared war against universal theories. They emphasized heterogeneity, with meaning being subjective and metaphoric, and arising from dialogue, as if nothing has greater validity than anything else. Mysticism and the occult are seen by some as having as much value as the accepted rational standards of society and the truths of science.

When anarchic individualism is worshipped, it is associated with a rejection of the values that form our society. The increase in violence and crime are also associated with anarchic individualism, where alienation from society occurs. In anarchic individualism violence is usually against an individual; in the symbiotic survival pattern it is usually against another group. However, both demonstrate a lack of regard for and a dehumanization of others.

Neither of these extremes is adaptive for men, neither loss of individual responsibility by submersion in a group nor abdication of social responsibility by extreme anarchic individualism. In the symbiotic survival pattern, group protection against feeling victimized is accomplished by the use of the defenses of splitting and projective identification. The outside enemy group is seen as all bad, and is held responsible for their misfortune. The scapegoated group can be a single group or a combination of groups, such as women, immigrants, minorities, or even the government. This paranoid thinking results in these men often feeling that there is a conspiracy against them. Frequently a paranoid leader is selected, who gains personal power by directing the anger against a scapegoated group. The scapegoated group can then be demonized and dehumanized, increasing the potential for violence against them.

Unfortunately, certain radical feminists also engage in a symbiotic survival pattern, and collectively see women as the victims of brutish men. These feminists also use splitting and stereotyping, seeing men as the all-bad enemy. All men are collectively considered as exploitative, controlling, unfeeling, and unable to establish intimate relationships. These radical feminists advance the stereotyped notion that all women are morally superior, empathic and more human, not operating by abstract rules, and able to relate better. This group of radical feminists, who engage in male bashing, tend to inflame the paranoia of many men against all other feminists and women in general.

Thus it is essential for the therapist to help the male patient become aware that there are many different groups of feminists, and not to also stereotype feminism by condemning all women who seek equality. The therapist needs to help men be able to retain their individuality and to see others as unique individuals. This may be hard to accomplish when some men feel insecure, threatened, and angry at the loss of inherited privilege. Polarization and paranoia by men or women does not resolve conflict, it only escalates the gender war.

## CONSTRICTION OF MEN
## BY MALE STEREOTYPES

Not only women, but men also have been constricted and
oppressed by the cultural gender role stereotypes. Men as
well as women have been victims of the culture. The therapist needs to help the patient become aware of the impact
of gender stereotyping that has constricted both sexes.
Male stereotypes have emphasized autonomy, competition, rationality, and self-sufficiency, with denial of human
attachment, cooperation, emotionality, and dependency.
The impact of this male gender stereotyping varies individually from man to man, with some men less influenced
than others.

The vulnerability of male gender identity with respect
to women is demonstrated in men's need to prove their
masculinity by performing sexually. Ethel Person (1980)
points out that if a man is impotent with a woman, his
sense of masculinity is often threatened, but a woman
can be inhibited or abstinent and still feel secure in her
femininity.

Karen Horney (1922) noted that many men have a neu-
rotic need for love and support, needing to dominate
and possess the female, and feeling enraged if they are
deprived or abandoned by a woman. On the other hand,
Betcher and Pollack (1993) speculate that many men recapitulate and master their dependency and the trauma
of separation from the preoedipal mother by repeatedly
loving and leaving women in adult life. Sex resurrects the
memories of physical touch, warmth, and nurturance of
early childhood with mother, as well as the need to separate in order to establish a male gender identity.

Meth and Pasick (1990) note that many men lead relatively isolated lives, with few intimate friends, because they are obsessed with work and need to fulfill the gender role of breadwinner to feel masculine. They may share camaraderie and bond with other men around a common activity, such as sports or drinking, but even there may lack real openness, sharing, and empathy.

Although women can relieve men of the burden of being the sole breadwinner, many men fear that economic empowerment of women represents a threat to their masculinity. Despite having monopolized the power and privilege that accompany being the provider, the man was also enslaved by his work. Working long hours often deprived him of emotional support from male friends and his wife, and he could not enjoy being a father to his children.

The therapist, therefore, needs to encourage the male patient to establish male friendships so that he has an emotional support network. In addition, sharing the load of economic responsibility with his wife does not mean she will dominate and emasculate him. Men do not need to dominate women to feel masculine, but can adopt a new male role involving intimacy and sharing that leads to true friendship with women. By also sharing childrearing, they can enjoy some of its many pleasures and contribute to their happiness.

## ANGER AND AGGRESSION

Anger and aggression have been the main outlet for some men to express all their emotions, since they empower a sense of maleness but do not expose their vulnerability. The opposite is true for many women, where the culture inhibits the expression of anger and aggression. For men there has been a cultural taboo about verbalizing caring or tender feelings for other men, as if such a man is not manly or is possibly homosexual. Thus many men feel free to express caring for other males only physically, through playful aggression or verbal teasing. Many men can physically express intimacy to women only through sex, and this cultural inhibition of emotions also limits men in their relationships with women. Many women cannot find emotional intimacy with men and turn to other women to share their inner experiences, resulting in the exclusion of men. The male cultural stereotype has therefore tended to alienate the sexes. Men need to learn to express all their feelings and learn to talk about their experiences, difficulties, and problems to be able to be more intimate and to receive emotional support.

## THERAPY WITH MEN

Ross (1992) notes that because of the learned restrictive influences of gender stereotyping, many men have found it difficult to enter therapy, to be open and admit they need help from a therapist. This is experienced by many men as an admission of failure, weakness, and an insult to their sense of masculinity. However, women do not have a monopoly on feelings, intimacy, or social skills. Men can become more complete human beings, and reown aspects of themselves that were split off. They can be bonded to their wives and children more closely, and can express their feelings openly without shame or suffering an identity crisis. The following is an outline of the steps to accomplish this in therapy.

## Engagement

The first problem with many men is to help them become *engaged* in the therapeutic process. Since many men have difficulty admitting problems and need to be in control, the therapist must be sensitive to this issue. It is important for the therapist not to offer help or suggestions in resolving problems without being asked to do so, which may threaten many men's sense of masculinity. The therapist needs to listen, so that the patient feels he is empathically heard but not patronized. Thus the therapist serves as a model of empathic connection with others for the male patient.

Establishing a *safe holding environment* is necessary for the patient to feel secure enough to lower his defenses and openly discuss his problems. The therapist needs to verbally acknowledge and bring to the surface the difficulty that many male patients have in seeking professional help. If the therapist *universalizes* this issue, the male patient does not suffer a loss of self-esteem, feel weak or a failure as a man. He is not alone, since many men also feel that they should be totally independent and the master of all situations like the lone cowboy in the movies. The therapist can say that most of us are not in total control of all situations, and to believe this is an idealized myth or illusion. There are many circumstances in life over which we have no control. Denying this robs the individual of the opportunity to face and emotionally work through his problems and to achieve a sense of mastery and wholeness.

If the therapist redefines the new role of masculinity, greater emotional freedom is permitted for the male patient. Women are not emotionally superior to men, and men have the same human potential for emotionality. But, by internalizing the older, restrictive stereotype of what it means to be male, this side of many men has been repressed. This cuts them off emotionally from themselves and from others. Men can now feel free to discuss their feelings and work them through together with the therapist to feel more whole and alive.

## Therapeutic Alliance

Establishing a *therapeutic alliance* next is essential, so that the patient can split his ego and observe himself also through the eyes of the therapist. The patient can then view himself and his issues from another perspective. For this alliance to be established, the patient needs to trust the therapist and to identify with the therapist's perspective. Thus the male patient can recognize that by joining with the therapist he has other options open to him on how to see, define, and react to a situation.

## Focus on Relationships, Not Simply Solutions

Men can also *learn to empathically listen* to their wives, allow them to express their emotionality and be connected, instead of offering rational solutions as described by John Gray (1992) in *Men Are from Mars, Women Are from Venus.* Men can thereby become more aware of the relationship and be less goal or task oriented. The man must achieve a balance between his collective identity as a male and his individual identity as a human being connected to other human beings.

Simply telling a man not to offer solutions, however, may not be enough. For a man to be able to empathize with his wife or female companion genuinely, he also needs to accept and be *aware of his own feelings*. If he denies his own feelings, he will tend to do the same to the emotions of women. When a woman expresses her feelings, he may condemn or shame her for being emotional, and the woman may feel inhibited about expressing and sharing her emotions with the man again. If the man himself is goal oriented, telling a man not to be that way is usually not sufficient. It is like telling someone to pull themselves up by their bootstraps, but the man does not even know where to reach. Repressing emotions is a deeply ingrained pattern, and has been internalized during childhood from cultural male stereotypes. It is, therefore, important to help the male in therapy to get in touch with his anxiety, sadness, grief, and other human feelings.

## Identifying and Differentiating Feelings

One of the most important tasks for the therapist is to help the patient identify, differentiate, and own the various feelings he experiences. Instead of expressing all his feelings through anger, denying or avoiding them, or externalizing and acting them out physically, he can learn what he is feeling underneath the mantle of anger. Men can thus differentiate their own feelings, learn to contain and integrate them, and to express them verbally. The therapist can help the patient not to feel ashamed of tender and loving feelings or of feeling helpless or pained.

Many men are more prone to develop post-traumatic stress disorder, since they may repress their feelings and not verbally work through the trauma they experienced. By erecting defenses against their feelings, they may become like living dead men and lose connection with themselves and others. Not only have they suffered a trauma, but others may feel excluded and in turn reject them, creating further trauma. By verbalizing their feelings about the incident, and working through their emotions, these men remain in touch with themselves and others, and do not suffer the secondary consequence of being rejected by those who were formerly close to them.

Human existence is always laced with painful events. None of us is immune to becoming physically ill or safe from accidents or illnesses happening to those we love. Men are particularly vulnerable now to economic insecurity as we change to a post-industrial society. A man can be fired from a job as he gets older or as a company is downsizing. Most men in the workplace have limited power, and are controlled by and accountable to authorities above them. Low-level white- or blue-collar male workers have always had little or no power over others and struggle just to get by.

The changing role structure of modern society has left many men confused and insecure even about how to behave appropriately. By escaping into alcohol, drugs, food, sex, gambling, sports, or work, men can avoid feeling anxious and depressed. These feelings, however, persist and, unless openly faced and worked through verbally, can have self-destructive consequences. The therapist can reframe how a man can be truly masculine. True male strength is achieved not by avoiding but by confronting and resolving painful feelings.

## Interpreting Interaction

Although the following phases of therapy have been previously discussed, it would be valuable to recapitulate them briefly.

Often individuals are unaware of the effects they have on others, and in turn how others influence them. At times men competitively need to demonstrate how much they know in order to prove their worth. A woman may experience this as an effort to take over and dominate a situation, and in response, she may react with anger or withdrawal. This may then produce a defensive reaction in the man, since he feels demeaned. Thus a tense stalemate results that most often goes unresolved.

The underlying issue may be that the man feels basically insecure or unsure of himself, and feels he needs external confirmation of his worth by trying to impress others. Instead of the affirmation he seeks, however, others may experience him negatively. By highlighting this circular interaction, which does not work for the man, the underlying issue of his insecurity can be broached. Perhaps the man did not receive the affirmation from his father that he desired and has not developed a positive and secure male image of himself. Here the therapist can clarify the interaction, define what was wished to be gained, and describe its effect on others and the self.

## Interpreting Projective Identification

Split-off aspects of the self that have been placed into a woman through projective identification are interpreted. The goal is to have the patient *reown these split-off aspects* so that they are not projected and acted out interpersonally. In order to do this and avoid criticizing the patient, I have found the following procedure effective:

1. *Reframe* the purpose in a positive light so that the person who contains the projective identification and enacts it is now seen as a savior and not a scapegoat.
2. *Link* the projective identification with childhood relationships and cultural stereotypes.
3. *Clarify* the need to split off aspects of the self to sustain gender identity, security, and self-esteem.

## Termination

Having reowned split-off aspects of himself and no longer shackled by outdated male stereotypes, the patient is freer to *work through* past intrapsychic conflicts and present issues. Working through is not a onetime occurrence, but the same issues need to be repeated over and over again under different circumstances. This repetition seems to be necessary to cognitively and emotionally reprogram the existing circuits in his nervous system.

Resolution of the transference to the therapist allows the patient to differentiate the therapist from past or present significant others. Change is difficult and, not infrequently, patients experience a threat to their survival, fearing that some catastrophe will occur if they relinquish their previous mode of adaptation.

Termination is difficult for many patients, since it is a loss of a valued, intimate relationship. It may be associated with abandonment or death, even though the patient and the therapist mutually agree it is time to end. The

anger and mourning need to be worked through here as
well. There may be a regression and recurrence of old conflicts at the end of therapy, which need to be relived and
experienced verbally. When the therapist contains the
patient's negative and sad feelings, the patient experiences the therapist as a constant figure who does not
retaliate or reject him and helps him work through the
issues of separation.

The patient can then mourn the deficiencies in his parents and his relationships with them, accept their limitations, and achieve a more autonomous and related self.

# References

Antonovsky, A., and Lerner, M. J. (1959). Negro and white youth in Elmira. In *Discrimination and Low Incomes*, ed. A. Antonovsky and L. Larwin, pp. 103–146. Study of the New York State Commission Against Discrimination. New York: New School for Social Research.

Bernstein B. (1962). Social class, linguistic codes, and grammatical elements. *Language and Speech* 5:221–240.

Bernstein, J., and Mishel, L. (1995). *The State of Working America 1994–1995*. Washington, DC: Economic Policy Institute.

Betcher, R. W., and Pollack, W. S. (1993). *In a Time of Fallen Heroes: The Re-creation of Masculinity*. New York: Atheneum.

Bieber, T. B., and Bieber, I. (1968). Resistance to marriage. In *The Marriage Relationship*, ed. S. Rosenbaum and I. Alger. New York: Basic Books.

Bly, R. (1990). *Iron John*. New York: Addison-Wesley.

Booth, A., Shelley, G., Mazur, A., et al. (1989). Testosterone and winning and losing in human competition. *Hormones and Behavior* 23:556–571.

Burton, R .V., and Whiting, J. W. M. (1961). The absent father and cross-sex identity. *Merrill Palmer Quarterly* 7:85–95.

Clark, K. B. (1964). *Youth in the Ghetto: A Study of the Consequences of Powerlessness and a Blueprint for Change*. New York: Harlem Youth Opportunities Unlimited Inc.

Clark, K. B., and Clark, M. P. (1950). Emotional factors in racial identification and preference in Negro children. *Journal of Negro Education* 19:341–350.

Dabbs, J. M., and Morris, R. (1990). Testosterone, social class and antisocial behavior in a sample of 4,462 men. *Psychological Science* 1:209–211.

de Beauvoir, S. (1961). *The Second Sex*. New York: Bantam Books.

Dinnerstein, D. (1976). *The Mermaid and the Minotaur*. New York: Harper and Row.

Durant, W. (1927). *The Story of Philosophy*. New York: Simon and Schuster.

Elshtain, J. (1994). *Democracy on Trial*. New York: Basic Books.

Erikson, E. H. (1963). *Childhood and Society*. New York: Norton.

Federal Glass Ceiling Commission Report (1995). *Good for Business: Making Field Use of the Nation's Human Capital*. Washington, DC: US Labor Department, U.S. Government Printing Office.

Freud, S. (1931). Female sexuality. *Standard Edition* 21.

Friedan, B. (1963). *The Feminine Mystique*. New York: Norton.

——— (1981). *The Second Stage*. New York: Summit.

Gay, J. (1995). The legless angel of David Copperfield: there is more to her than Victorian piety. *New York Times Book Review*, January 22, pp. 22–24.

Gay, P. (1988). *Freud: A Life for Our Time*. New York: Norton.

Goleman, D. (1995). An elusive picture of violent men who kill mates. *New York Times*, January 15, p. 22.

Greenberg, S. (1980). An experimental study of under-achievement: the effects of subliminal merging and success-related stimuli on the academic performance of bright, underachieving high school students. Ph.D. dissertation, New York University.

Greenson, R. R. (1968). Dis-identifying from mother: its special importance for the boy. *International Journal of Psycho-Analysis* 49:370–374.

Gray, J. (1992). *Men Are from Mars, Women Are from Venus*. New York: Harper Collins.

Grünbaum, A. (1993). *Validation in the Clinical Theory of Psychoanalysis: A Study in the Philosophy of Psychoanalysis*. New York: International Universities Press.

Harlow, H. F. (1958). The nature of love. *American Psychologist* 13:673–685.

Harrington, M. (1962). *The Other America*. Baltimore, MD: Penguin.

Herzog, E. (1966). Is there a "breakdown" of the Negro family? *Social Work* 11:3–10.

Hollingshead, A. B., and Redlich, F. C. (1958). *Social Class and Mental Illness*. New York: Wiley.

Horney, K. (1922). On the genesis of the castration complex in women. In *Feminine Psychology*, ed. H. Kelman, p. 38. New York: Norton, 1967.

Johnson, R. (1957). Negro reactions to minority group status. In *American Minorities*, ed. M. L. Barron, pp. 192–212. New York: Knopf.

Johnson, A. M., and Szurek, S. A. (1954). Ideology of anti-social behavior in delinquents and psychopaths. *Journal of the American Medical Association* 154:814–817.

Johnston, J. (1992). Why Iron John is no gift to women. *New York Times Book Review*, February 23, pp. 1, 28, 29, 31, 33.

Jung, C. G. (1959). Archetypes of the collective unconscious. *Collected Works*, vol. 9. New York: Bollingen.

Kardiner, A., and Ovesey, L. (1951). *The Mark of Oppression*. New York: Norton.

Kaufman, W. (1974). *Nietzsche: Philosopher, Psychologist, Anti-Christ*. Princeton, NJ: Princeton University Press.

Kernberg, O. F. (1976). *Object Relations Theory and Clinical Psychoanalysis*. New York: Jason Aronson.

——— (1986). Identification and its vicissitudes as observed in psychosis. *International Journal of Psycho-Analysis* 67:147–159.

Komarovsky, M. (1940). *The Unemployed Man and His Family*. New York: Holt, Rinehart, and Winston.

Langner, T. S., and Michael, S. T. (1963). *Life Stress and Mental Health*. Glencoe, IL: Free Press.

Leighton, A. H. (1959). *My Name Is Legion*. New York: Basic Books.

——— (1965). Poverty and social change. *Scientific American*, 212:21–27.

Lewis, O. (1959). *Five Families*. New York: Basic Books.

——— (1961). *The Children of Sanchez*. New York: Random House.

——— (1966). *La Vida*. New York: Random House.

Lidz, T., and Lidz, R. (1988). *Oedipus in the Stone Age*. New York: International Universities Press.

Lorenz, K. (1966). *On Aggression*. New York: Harcourt, Brace, and World.

Maccoby, E. E., and Jacklin, C. N. (1974). *The Psychology of Sex Differences*. Palo Alto, CA: Stanford University Press.

Malinowski, R. (1929). *The Sexual Life of Savages*. New York: Harcourt, Brace, and World.

McGoldrick, M., Pearce, J. K., and Giordano, J. (1982). *Ethnicity and Family Therapy*. New York: Guilford.

Merton, R. K. (1957). Social structure and anomie. In *Social Theory and Social Structure*, pp. 131–150. Glencoe, IL: Free Press.

Meth, R. L., and Pasick, R. S. (1990). *Men in Therapy*. New York: Guilford.

Milner, E. (1953). Some hypotheses concerning the influence of segregation on Negro personality development. *Psychiatry* 16:291–297.

Minuchin, S. (1964). *Family structure, family language, and the puzzled therapist*. Paper presented at the 41st annual meeting, American Orthopsychiatric Association, March.

Noble, B. P. (1994). Now he's stressed, she's stressed. *New York Times*, October 9, p. 21.

Person, E. S. (1980). Sexuality as the mainstay of identity: psychoanalytic perspectives. In *Women, Sex, and Sexuality*, ed. C. R. Stimpson and E. S. Person, pp. 36–61. Chicago: University of Chicago Press.

Pettigrew, T. F. (1964). *A Profile of the Negro American*. Princeton, NJ: Van Nostrand.

Pittman, F. (1992). Family therapy and the death of patriarchy. *Family Therapy News*. 23:9, 25. American Association of Marriage and Family Therapy.

Rainwater, L. (1966). Crucible of identity: the Negro lower-class family. *Daedalus* 95:172–216.

Rodman, H. (1968). Family and social pathology in the ghetto. *Science* 161:756–762.

Ross, J. M. (1992). *The Male Paradox*. New York: Simon and Schuster.

Salk, L. (1990). Raising boys, raising girls. *McCall's,* December, pp. 84–86.

Scanzoni, J. (1967). Socialization, achievement, and achievement values. *American Sociology Review* 32:449–456.

Scheflen, A. E. (1963). Communication and regulation in psychotherapy. *Psychiatry* 26:126–136.

——— (1964). The significance of posture in communication systems. *Psychiatry* 27:316–331.

Schorske, C. E. (1981). *Fin-de-Siècle Vienna: Politics and Culture.* New York: Vintage.

Silverman, L. H. (1975). On the role of laboratory experiments in the development of the clinical theory of psychoanalysis. *International Review of Psycho-Analysis* 2:43–64.

Slipp, S. (1969). The psychotic adolescent in the context of the family. Presented at the annual meeting of the American Medical Association, and printed in *The Emotionally Troubled Adolescent and the Family Physician,* ed. M. G. Kalogerakis, pp. 229–239. Springfield, IL: Charles C Thomas, 1973.

——— (1973). The symbiotic survival pattern: a relational theory of schizophrenia. *Family Process* 12:377–398.

——— (1984). *Object Relations: A Dynamic Bridge Between Individual and Family Treatment.* New York: Jason Aronson.

——— (1988). *The Technique and Practice of Object Relations Family Therapy.* Northvale, NJ: Jason Aronson.

——— (1993). *The Freudian Mystique.* New York: New York University Press.

——— (1994). Family therapy and multiple-family therapy. In *Comprehensive Textbook of Group Psychotherapy,*

ed. H. I. Kaplan and B. J. Sadock, pp. 270–283. Baltimore, MD: Williams and Wilkins.

Slipp, S., and Nissenfeld, S. (1981). An experimental study
of psychoanalytic theories of depression. *Journal
of the American Academy of Psychoanalysis* 9:583–
600.

Spinley, B. M. (1953). *The Deprived and the Privileged:
Personality Development in English Society*. London:
Routledge and Kegan Paul.

Srole, L., Langner, T. S., Michael, S. T., et al. (1961). *Mental Health in the Metropolis, The Midtown Manhattan Study*, vol. 1. Thomas A. C. Rennie Series in Social Psychiatry. New York: McGraw-Hill.

Stern, D. N. (1985). *The Interpersonal World of the Infant*.
New York: Basic Books.

Stoller, R. J. (1968). *Sex and Gender*. New York: Science
House.

Stone, M. H. (1981). Borderline syndromes: a consideration of subtypes and an overview: directions for research. *Psychiatric Clinics of North America* 4:3–24.
——— (1988). *The Fate of the Borderline*. New York: Guilford Press.

Terry, D. (1994). Two brothers held in slaying of a murder suspect. *New York Times*, September 3, p. 6, Section A.

U.S. Census Bureau Report (1992). U.S. Department of
Commerce and Economics, Statistics Administration,
Bureau of the Census, Washington, DC: U.S. Government Printing Office.

Van der Kolk, B. (1986). *Psychological Trauma*. Washington, DC: American Psychiatric Press.

Veblen, T. (1899). *The Theory of the Leisure Class*. New
York: Modern Library, 1934.

Wallerstein, J. S., and Kelly, J. B. (1980). *Surviving The Breakup: How Children and Parents Cope with Divorce.* New York: Basic Books.

Wittenberg, R. H. (1948). Personality adjustment through social action. *American Journal of Orthopsychiatry* 18:207–221.

# Index